GEORGE GISSING
AND H. G. WELLS

THE H. G. WELLS PAPERS
AT THE UNIVERSITY OF ILLINOIS

General Editor: Gordon N. Ray

Henry James and H. G. Wells
Edited by Leon Edel and Gordon N. Ray

Arnold Bennett and H. G. Wells
Edited by Harris Wilson

George Gissing and H. G. Wells
Edited by Royal Gettmann

IN PREPARATION

Bernard Shaw and H. G. Wells
Edited by Gordon N. Ray

'Promised by the shores of Devon,
In the Springtime, 'ninety-seven,
George Gissing
July 12, 1897'

GEORGE GISSING

AND

H. G. WELLS

Their Friendship
and Correspondence

Edited with an Introduction by
Royal A. Gettmann

UNIVERSITY OF ILLINOIS PRESS
Urbana, 1961

Printed in Great Britain by Richard Clay and Company, Ltd.
Bungay, Suffolk

FOR

M. H. Black

CONTENTS

ILLUSTRATIONS

PREFACE

THE quality and value of George Gissing's letters have been appraised in Virginia Woolf's statement that they "have character . . . little wit and no brilliance" but that in reading them "we feel that we are filling in a design" of the novels. In other words, no single novel of Gissing's wholly satisfies us; yet we respect him and wish to know more about him as a writer and as a man. The letters in the present volume reveal an aspect of him, and of Wells too, that did not come out clearly in Wells's writings about Gissing. Some admirers of Gissing have felt that in *Experiment in Autobiography* Wells's attitude toward him was tinged with coldness and even hostility. And it is true that the final paragraph on Gissing begins, "So ended all that flimsy inordinate stir of grey matter that was George Gissing." But it may be that Wells was simply perplexed by the life and career of his friend and also that he was weary of the Gissing problem. His attempt to enhance Gissing's reputation and his prolonged efforts to help Gissing's brother, sons, and widow had met with petty objections and interference. However that may be, the letters reveal respect and sympathy and responsiveness on the part of both men.

The holographs of these letters are in the Wells Collection at the University of Illinois. They are now printed for the first time, though Morley Roberts, who used them when he was writing *The Private Life of Henry Maitland*, quoted twenty-eight sentences from nine letters. Inasmuch as five of these sentences are from a letter that is missing from the Wells Collection, it cannot be claimed that the Gissing letters are quite complete. Only one envelope has survived. In the notes there are numerous quotations from and references to letters by acquaintances of Gissing and Wells. Unless otherwise indicated all these are in the Wells Collection.

It is a pleasure to acknowledge the assistance given me by everyone I consulted in the course of my work. Mr A. C. Gissing and Madame Denise Le Mallier graciously gave me permission to publish the letters. Mrs Charles Shattuck, who sifted and arranged the mass of material in the Wells Collection, put me on the track of some elusive persons mentioned in the letters. Gordon N. Ray, Provost and Vice-President of the University of Illinois, permitted me to use a letter from Wells to Gosse. Mr Brian Ború Dunne not only identified himself but generously supplied me with his vivid memories of Gissing. For other help of various kinds, expertly and willingly given, I am indebted to Miss Alma DeJordy, Miss Eva Faye Benton, Paul Haines, Jacob Korg, George Goodin, and Louis Tsen. I thank Jack Stillinger for help on the proof. My greatest obligation is to my wife, whose help went far beyond the typing of the manuscript.

Urbana, Illinois R. A. G.
February 1961

INTRODUCTION

THE dinner of the Omar Khayyám Club at Frascati's on 20 November 1896, brought together for the first time two men whose experience of life and attitude of mind were parallel at several points. Both George Gissing and H. G. Wells had been born in the lower social rank. Gissing's father conducted a comparatively successful chemist's shop at Wakefield in Yorkshire, and Wells's father half-heartedly kept a crockery shop at Bromley in Kent. Both men had dined with Poverty. During his early years in London Gissing had often fared on bread, dripping, and desiccated soup; Wells, as a student at the Normal School of Science in South Kensington, had been obliged to count his coins outside small fried-fish shops. Both had been depressed by quarters in Westbourne Park, a deteriorating, sub-letting section of London, and both had resorted to the Reading Room of the British Museum for light, shelter, and comfort. Each had made a trial of teaching: Gissing in a Massachusetts high school and in private tutoring in London, and Wells, after escaping from an apprenticeship in the Southsea Drapery Emporium, in a dismal academy in Wales. Both felt that religion was no longer a useful embodiment of human knowledge or a source of new light: they were even hostile toward formal religious groups. Gissing and Wells were critical of, or perhaps more accurately, discontented with the organisation of society and the state of culture. Under the influence of Positivism Gissing declared in 1880 that he meant to expose the "ghastly condition" of the poor classes and the "hideous injustice" of the whole social system. Five years later Wells wore a red tie to signalise his faith in socialism. Both had been subject to the imperious thrust of sexual longings, had experienced unhappy marriages and had married for a second time. And finally, both had resolved to make their living and their name by their pens.

Although the outlines of the experiences and general attitudes of Gissing and Wells were similar, the details and the final shading were different. Gissing slowly achieved a qualified success with a limited audience, whereas Wells rushed to prosperity and world-wide fame. As Wells relates his story in *Experiment in Autobiography*, his life was not a struggle upstream but a dexterous manipulation of the eddies and currents which exhausted and finally overwhelmed Gissing. The very things—love, marriage, and ill-health—that Gissing had to contend against caught up Wells and carried him to fresh opportunities and successes. This is forcibly brought out at one point in the autobiography when Wells pauses for a summary statement: "I have already explained how I became one of the intelligentsia and was saved from a limited life behind a draper's counter by two broken legs, my own first, and then my father's. I have now to tell how I was guided to mental emancipation and real prosperity by a smashed kidney, a ruptured pulmonary blood vessel, an unsuccessful marriage, and an uncontrollable love affair."

It is quite clear that Gissing caught the attention and claimed the admiration of women. And it is also clear that he was attentive to women. That is apparent from passages in a number of letters in the Wells Collection, of which one from Mrs Popham to Mrs Wells is typical. Referring to her recently published book, she wrote, "I have had a charming letter from Gissing to whom I sent a copy. He couldn't have said anything nasty of course but politeness did not demand anything so encouraging." In his novels Gissing repeatedly tested a man's character by appraising his response to a woman. Although Arnold Jacks, in *The Crown of Life*, is full of ardent notions about the expansion of the British Empire, he is incapable of passion for Irene Derwent. In the presence of her beauty and sensibility "he had not the least thought of engaging deeper emotion." Similarly, though Dyce Lashmar, in *Our Friend the Charlatan*, uses the influence of several women in his dishonest attempt to enter politics, he cunningly avoids any kind of emotional engagement. Not until the final pages—and only after Iris Woolston has paid tribute to his ego with fulsome praise—does he show any feeling. And even then Gissing condemns him with the words, "his amorous countenance had an undernote of thoughtfulness." In short, Dyce

Lashmar is despicable because he cannot give or receive love. Gissing's attraction for women and his response to them are reflected in his gallery of feminine characters which, as William Plomer has pointed out, is remarkable for variety, subtlety, and depth of understanding.

But despite Gissing's good looks, courtesy, and his high regard for love, his own marriages brought him misery, pain, disease, and guilt. At the age of nineteen he fell in love with a Manchester prostitute; and in an effort to help her, he committed a number of thefts in the cloakroom of Owens College. Sent to America for a year, he returned in 1877 and rejoined Nell, whom he married in 1879. After a short period of precarious happiness the marriage became a torment through poverty, Nell's poor health, and Gissing's frustration. By 1881 Nell was seriously ill from tuberculosis and alcoholism. In 1885 she returned to the streets, and Gissing never saw her again until he was called in 1888 to a slum in Lambeth where she had died alone. Three years later Gissing married again but soon found himself afflicted by domestic discomfort which shortly worsened until it became marital discord that could only be resolved by separation. At the age of forty-two Gissing attracted and returned the love of Gabrielle Fleury, a woman with whom he found happiness, but he was afflicted by a querulous mother-in-law, poverty, a breakdown in his health, and, not least, by his expatriation in France.

Wells's story is quite another thing. The first marriage

was simply a disappointment. As a student he had "tethered" his "sexual and romantic imagination" to a gentle, low-pitched cousin and, in his own words, that attachment, "quite as much as my poverty, saved me from the squalor of the street-walker." When his glittering hopes of love were dimmed, Wells left his wife, with relative painlessness on both sides, and arranged an adequate alimony. He married one of his students whose humour, good sense, and understanding made this union a partnership which allowed him to exercise in other attachments his very considerable sexual prowess. Indeed, Wells's escape from his inauspicious first marriage into the happiness and freedom of his second was the reverse of the misery, shame, and frustration which befell Gissing in his marriages.

Since money—or rather the lack of it—is one of the persistent themes in Gissing's novels, it will not be amiss to compare the financial positions of Wells and Gissing at the time of their first meeting. In 1896, his fourth year as a professional writer, Wells's income was £1056. 7s. 9d., whereas Gissing, after sixteen years of publishing novels, earned £289. 13s. 7d. Gissing's income was not only low: it fluctuated to a nerve-racking degree. In 1894, his banner year, it had risen to £453, and the margin between this sum and his expenditure of £239 caused Gissing to conclude his diary for the year with the word *Bravo*. But in 1897 Gissing's earnings dropped disastrously to £101. 13s. 4d.

The reason for the very different financial situations of the two men was their divergent attitudes towards journalistic writing. Wells began his career in journalism, whereas Gissing's first venture was *Workers in the Dawn*, a novel of proletarian life which, in the heyday of such titles as *Goodbye, Sweetheart!*, *Dr Cupid*, and *Fallen Leaves*, he had to publish at his own expense. In other words, Wells did not have to come to terms with journalism: he positively welcomed it. In *Experiment in Autobiography* he recalled how he accidentally hit upon the "true path" to journalistic success when, recuperating from a serious illness, he stumbled upon a passage by J. M. Barrie to the effect that editors did not want "views on politics" or "reflections on art" or "theories of life." Instead they welcomed lively pieces on flower-pots and tobacco-pipes. After quoting the passage Wells commented, "Why had I never thought in that way before? For years I had been seeking rare and precious topics. *Rediscovery of the Unique! Universe Rigid!* . . . All the time I had been shooting over the target. All I had to do was to lower my aim—and hit." The success with which Wells dropped his sights and hit the mark is clear from the books he published in 1895—four of them (two within a day of each other), all bearing the imprint of reputable publishers, and three of the four compiled from pieces he had written for newspapers and magazines during the preceding three years. In 1896 Wells was commanding fifty shillings for a book-review of a thousand words and seven guineas a thousand for what he called "invented things." Wells attributed his swift advance in journalism to his "facetious Destiny." But almost any page of his work will show that his success was not a matter of simple good luck but that it resulted from a quick, shifting curiosity, a temperament and sensibility not too fine for the workaday world, a wonderful zest for language and the capacity to convey that pleasure, and a high opinion of his chance of success. If Wells's confidence sometimes verged upon self-conceit, it nevertheless served to turn his thoughts outward and to keep his mind and interests flexible.

Gissing lacked that kind of confidence, though he had an ample fund of dogged perseverance and of pride, somewhat tinged with a desire for respectability. These qualities tended to draw him inward, and they caused him to keep aloof from journalism and made him half disdainful of it—but only half. In *New Grub Street* he ridiculed the career-mongering of Whelpdale, who had made a fantastic success of *Chat* by brightening the title to *Chit-Chat*, reducing all the articles to a length of two inches, and insisting that "every inch must be broken into at least two paragraphs." (Interestingly enough, Wells had made his beginning with a contribution to *Tit-Bits*.) But even though Gissing was contemptuous of Whelpdale's writing and editing, he allowed him to be generous and sensitive as a man. Certainly there is no suggestion in the letters in the present volume that Gissing looked askance at Wells's work as a journalist. In *The Private Papers of Henry Ryecroft* ("Summer," XXIII) Gissing expressed pleasure in Wells's financial prosperity and social success and praised his response to them—his avoidance of "busyness," his refusal to write down to the "baser throng," his preservation of a margin of privacy, and his continued enthusiasm for books old and new. Nevertheless there was a degree of difference between the two men: Wells was a writer whereas Gissing was a novelist.

It was not want of ability that kept Gissing from journalism. Although he lacked Wells's easy gaiety with words, he had the necessary competence: that much is clear from his writing of a piece on Battersea Bridge. Loitering by the Thames one evening in the autumn of 1883 he was struck by a glorious sunset. Hurrying home he wrote a description of what he had seen, posted it forthwith to a newspaper, and saw it in print the next morning. Recalling the incident in *The Private Papers of Henry Ryecroft* ("Autumn," XXI), Gissing significantly concluded, "I wrote it because I enjoyed doing so, quite as much as because I was hungry." And Gissing's ability on this plane is emphatically clear in *By the Ionian Sea*, in which his personality and the topography and historical information are nicely adjusted—without tasteless self-display, strained brightness, or gratuitous learning. The book is an appealing blend of fluctuations in thought and mood and a delineation of the contours of concrete reality. There was no reason why Gissing should have waited until 1899 to write such a book as *By the Ionian Sea*.

Nor was it lack of opportunity that kept Gissing from journalism. In 1880 he contributed two articles on socialism to the *Pall Mall Gazette*; and John Morley, the editor, wanted further work from him. The same year Gissing accepted an invitation to write the British articles for the Russian quarterly, *Le Messager de l'Europe*. But by the summer of 1882 he described this work as "most hideous" and "loathsome." No doubt this potting up of materials sifted from newspapers and parliamentary debates was tedious, but the reason Gissing gave it up was that by this time his enthusiasm for Positivism and his concern for political problems had waned. In view of the number, variety, and excellence of British periodicals being published at that time, and in view of the fact that the editors were more receptive and open-minded than the publishers of novels, it might be argued that Gissing, in holding aloof from them, not only deprived himself of extra income but cut himself off from the stimulus of an immediate audience, literary friendships, and the aid of editors. The argument is pointless, for it is too simple to say that he was deterred by stubbornness and pride. It was rather a question of sincerity: Gissing could not write unless he was interested, and his interests were not so wide or so easily engaged as were those of Wells.

It has been suggested that in 1893 Gissing relaxed his

standards somewhat when, having failed in repeated attempts to finish a novel, he accepted an invitation to write stories and sketches for weekly papers. Two years later, so the suggestion runs, he yielded a bit further as a result of a holiday at the Aldeburgh home of Edward Clodd. Among the guests was Grant Allen, who had employed his facile pen on books as different as *Physiological Aesthetics*, *For Maimie's Sake: A Tale of Love and Dynamite*, and *The Woman Who Did*. Another member of the house-party was Clement Shorter, who improved the occasion by commissioning Gissing to write six stories and twenty sketches for the *Illustrated London News* and the *Sketch*. It may be that Gissing's acquaintance with this circle caused him to be more tolerant of the kind of literary work and popularity that he had bitterly smiled at in *New Grub Street* and *In the Year of Jubilee*. And, incidentally, it perhaps made him more ready for his friendship with Wells. But even though Gissing may have become more sympathetic with what Jasper Milvain, in *New Grub Street*, described as "good, coarse marketable stuff for the world's vulgar," he did not waver in his own attitude toward literature. On occasion he spoke slightingly of his short stories, but they were after all in the realm of imaginative writing. And though some of them were tired and thin, Gissing never used the short form to evade the problems of human nature, and he never wrote less well than he was able to do. Even in *Will Warburton*, the posthumously published novel in which Gissing acknowledged and came to terms with his social pride, there is no lessening of his high conception of art. He approved of his hero's finding happiness in the grocery trade, but he did not condone Norbert Frank's forsaking serious painting for lucrative fashionable portraiture. Gissing understood all too well the pressure of financial need to which the painter was subjected, but he nevertheless described the change in him as a deterioration and he charged it to the fact that Frank was "without enthusiasm for art." To Gissing this was unforgivable, for such was his own dedication to letters that even in his lowest moods he could still muster that enthusiasm. In short, Gissing devoted his life to the making of novels; and though they must be ranked below the masterpieces, they are different from them in degree, not in kind. In origin and purpose they are akin to the novels of Jane Austen and George Eliot. Wells, on the other hand, was a writer of novels, articles, prolegomena, and text-books. His gusto and inventiveness made them vastly entertaining, but his first purpose was to broach ideas, with aesthetic effects incidental.

Despite his allegiance to literature, his determination and industry, and his intelligent awareness of the personal and social problems of his time, Gissing never quite succeeded in writing a thoroughly good novel. His lack of final success was partly a matter of craftsmanship—a failure to concentrate and dramatise. It was what Frederic Harrison had in mind when he said of *Workers in the Dawn*, "There is enough stuff in the book to make six novels." And it was no doubt one of the reasons why Meredith urged Gissing to reduce *Isabel Clarendon* from three volumes to two. Gissing himself was aware of the problem. In 1885, about the time the circulating libraries delivered their ultimatum against the three-decker, Gissing declared, "It is fine to see how the old three volume tradition is being broken through. One volume is becoming commonest of all. It is the new school, due to continental influence. Thackeray and Dickens wrote at enormous length, and with profusion of detail. . . . Far more artistic, I think, is the later method, of merely suggesting; of dealing with episodes, instead of writing biographies. . . . In fact, it approximates to the dramatic mode of presentment." This was not a passing observation gathered from his reading of Turgenev at this time: years later he wrote, "Dickens never had command of 'situation,' though he was strong in incident. A great situation must be *led* up to by careful and skilful foresight." Yet this was the very thing that disturbed Henry James, who, despite a "persistent taste" for Gissing's novels, was compelled to admit his repeated disappointment in them. James could explain his dissatisfaction only as follows, "The whole business of distribution and composition he strikes me as having cast to the winds."

In suggesting that Gissing was indifferent to the whole problem of composition James was less than fair. It was not simply a matter of knowledge or effort or technical competence: it was rather a question of ability and temperament. With his turn of mind and with the emotional tensions caused by his experience, Gissing was deficient in what, for lack of a better term, may be called the sympathetic imagination. He could not wholly lose himself in his characters; hence, unable to expand and dramatise his crucial situations, he resorted to the multiplication of episodes and characters and to the extension of illustrative talk.

The problem appears in the prose style of Gissing. On many of his pages one does not sense the pressure of a state of mind or of emotion behind the sentences, because Gissing was unable to immerse himself in alien attitudes and feelings. The result is a kind of neutral, formal style which makes the dialogue stiff and not quite credible. (Thus the conversations between Piers and his father in *The Crown of Life* are not so effective as their letters—that is, the formalities of letter-writing lend a plausibility to the bookishness of style.) Passages which rise above clarity and competence—and they are more numerous than is commonly supposed—are likely to be those which express the thrust of Gissing's private concerns, as for example in the following, "The happy people of the world are the dull, unimaginative beings from whom the gods, in their kindness, have veiled all vision of the rising and the setting day, of sea-limits, and of the stars of the night, whose ears are thickened against the voice of music, whose thought finds nowhere mystery." Now this sentence should win sympathy for Thyrza, a talented, sensitive working-girl, but some readers will feel that it fails to do so. They will contend that Gissing did not identify himself with her—indeed that he did not even go so far as to use her for a mask. They will hear in this passage the overtones of pride and self-pity and gratuitous pessimism of Gissing's own voice. To borrow from Hazlitt's distinction between Shakespeare and Milton, Gissing did not transform himself into Thyrza but assigned to her his frustration, self-esteem, and resentment. If a reader is an enthusiast for the chameleon-like, withdrawn novelist and if he subscribes to the view that a literary work is autonomous and organic—divorced from author and audience—then he will be dissatisfied with more than a few pages of Gissing.

But the passage quoted was the essential Gissing: remove the sense of injustice and the note of wounded pride and bitter resignation from Gissing's novels and the result is a middling, merely competent story. Now a feeling of victimisation is not necessarily inimical to the success of a novel. If it is not simply a reflexive whimper or outcry, if the author is felt to be not a solitary sufferer but a representative of a considerable number of men, then his novel may be taken as a controlled rendering of a generalised moral interest and one deserving respect even though it may lack some of the oblique technical devices of recent fiction.

In a larger sense Gissing wavered with respect to his

overall purpose in the writing of fiction. He once declared, "My attitude henceforth is that of the artist pure and simple. The world is for me a collection of phenomena, which are to be studied and reproduced artistically." On another occasion he asserted, "Human life has little interest to me, on the whole—save as material for artistic presentation." But his dividedness appeared in the very next sentence, "I can get savage over social iniquities, but even then my rage at once takes the direction of planning revenge in artistic work." The titles of his novels—for example, *Born in Exile*, *In the Year of Jubilee*, *The Whirlpool*, *The Odd Women*—show that he could not harmonise his practice with his theory, that he could not assent to Wilde's avowal, "All art is quite useless."

But the question as to how a literary work is useful has long perplexed critics and writers, and the answers to it have been very different. For example, Dr Johnson, not wholly trustful of Shakespeare's "exhibition" of his characters, wished for a more emphatic enunciation of "precepts" and "axioms." On the other hand, Keats, though he wished to do some good for the world, suspected poetry with a palpable design and preferred the obliqueness of "To Autumn" and "Lamia." The kind of answer an author gives to this question depends in part upon his attitude toward his audience and his view of culture and society. From Coleridge onwards there were writers who protested against certain aspects of the nineteenth century, but in the early and middle decades they remained within the society they criticised. Toward the close of the century, however, there was an increasing tendency to regard society as alien and inhospitable. In the light of the rebelliousness shown by some writers and the retreat into private moods and the irresponsible aestheticism of others, the uncertainty of Gissing's theory and practice is at least free from cocksureness and over-simplification.

If Gissing was perplexed and uncertain in his conception of art, Wells was impatient with or perhaps bored by the whole question. From the first he was naturally opposed to what he called the "Weary Giant theory" of the novel—the easy notion that fiction was "wholly and solely a means of relaxation" for men after they had done their daily stint of the world's work. By 1911 he came to doubt Henry James's contention that the novel, too often a collection of characters strung together on a chain of episodes, should be refined into "an organized, moulded, balanced composition, gratifying the reader with a sense of design and construction." And in *Boon* (1915) Wells cried down James's theory and practice with such assertions as these: "But James has never discovered that a novel isn't a picture . . . that life isn't a studio. . . . He is the culmination of the Superficial type." Wells further declared that James's selection was "just omission and nothing more. . . . For example, he omits opinions." In Wells's view a praiseworthy novel was not a self-contained, anonymous object which subtly transfigured daily experience and public life for attentive, disciplined readers: it was a book that did things to people. And what it did was change "all the activities of the race" and unify "the collective thought of a community." The means of bringing about these social readjustments was the direct presentation of opinions. Wells advocated the very thing that Flaubert had condemned in his declaration, "As for expressing my opinion on the people I introduce, no, a thousand times no!" (Actually Flaubert did disclose his opinions: for example, he censured Emma by means of a page-long metaphor, and he denounced provincial society by way of a close description of a wedding-cake.) In short, James felt that Wells failed to master ideas and transmute them into imaginative forms of essential experience, and Wells charged James with evading ideas and problems.

The tastelessness of Wells's attack upon James in *Boon* has left the impression that the difference between the two men was a merely personal one: it has obscured the fact that their quarrel was also a manifestation of two attitudes toward the art of fiction. And the ease with which James scored his victory in the exchange of letters makes it difficult to defend Wells. Furthermore, the pervasive influence of James's Prefaces and the obvious defects in Wells's novels—which he described as "hurried and inadequately revised"—and his eventual desertion of fiction have squared with and contributed to the widely-held view that the only valid kind of novel is the closed, strictly focused one of Flaubert and James. But a characteristic utterance from D. H. Lawrence, "They want me to have form. That means, they want me to have *their* pernicious, ossiferous, skin-and-grief form, and I won't," suggests that there is another area in the province of fiction and that Wells was not the only worker in it.

In the light of such pairs of writers as Wilde and Kipling, Bennett and Virginia Woolf, Joyce and Lawrence, Gissing is seen as one of Wells's kind. Despite certain temperamental differences, the two had much in common, and they addressed themselves to the same questions. They were members of the first generation to have matured in the climate created by *On the Origin of Species*. They were separated from their elders by a break in religious belief and by the suspicion that literacy, self-interest, inventions, and commerce were not enough, that the confidence expressed in the Great Exhibition was not fulfilled by the Diamond Jubilee.

Both Gissing and Wells turned to science for the answers. In 1879 Gissing was poring over Comte, Buckle, and Huxley, and in December of that year he avowed, "Now my special study is social science . . . everything I read I make subservient to this aim—the acquisition of a knowledge of the history of society. As a would be novelist, I must necessarily work in this direction." Within a few years, certainly by 1883, Gissing's hope in the social sciences and mass-education waned, and in *In the Year of Jubilee* he ridiculed one of his characters who was equally enthusiastic about the novels of George Eliot and those of Mrs Henry Wood and who passed "from puerile facetiae . . . to speculations on the origin of being, and with an equally light heart." In this mood of disenchantment Gissing retreated in his very last years to the position of a withdrawn, sensitive man exercising his tastes and arranging his meditations in an atmosphere of vague ruralism untouched by science and trade. Wells naturally thought that such a conception of culture was hopelessly inadequate in a complex, urbanised society, and in his final word on the subject he declared that Gissing "spent his big fine brain deprecating life, because he would not and perhaps could not look life squarely in the eyes." As an estimate of Gissing's entire life this statement is unjust, but a clear-eyed reading of *The Private Papers of Henry Ryecroft* will endorse it as an appraisal of that book. (It should be remarked that the sympathetic treatment of Bladesover in *Tono-Bungay* shows Wells's appreciation of the cultural values of the country house, but he believed that the day of Bladesover was past.)

Perhaps Wells's dissatisfaction was sharpened by the fact that he and Gissing treated the same problems: the trials of the unclassed young man who has a good mind but a thin purse; the importance of money to a man's self-respect and self-fulfilment; the difficulty of establishing and maintaining a satisfactory relationship between a man and a woman—that is, an association that harmonises sexual passion, the need for enduring affection and intellectual compatibility, and difference in social position; the problem of a man's adjusting himself to a society which he disapproves of—that is, the difficulty of avoiding a negative withdrawal or a rebelliousness or a feeling of self-pity and self-punishment, or a dishonest adaptation; the dangers of jingoism and the threat of war; and finally the basic problem of authority—that is, who or what is responsible for the direction society should take in the confused stream of daily events.

But in the end the significance of Gissing's novels may have been more positive than Wells supposed, for the ultimate effect of imaginative works is not palpable and immediate. The quality of British patriotism may be taken as a case in point: the contentious jingoism of the nineties was entirely absent from the spirit of resistance and endurance shown during the Second World War. And who is to say that *In the Year of Jubilee* and *The Crown of Life* did not contribute to that modulation? To cite another example—the lowering of fences between classes and the extension of social services may be directly attributed to such factors as changes in modes of communication and transport and to the redistribution of wealth through the revision of taxes. But again, who is to say that these were not in some degree the realisation of the attitudes expressed in such novels as *Thyrza* and *The Nether World*? In respect to the development of the

English novel it must be admitted that Gissing did not open new doors upon unprecedented technical devices or unexplored subject-matter. He was a mediator between the Victorians, who emphasised social relationships, and the innovators of the 1920s, who concentrated on the individual consciousness. But whatever modifications the future may bring in taste and critical theory, at mid-century such a novel as *Born in Exile* still deserves the respect of serious students of English fiction.

I

GISSING TO WELLS

27 *November* 1896 *Eversley, Worple Road, Epsom*[1]

DEAR MR WELLS, Your letter contains the most amusing, the most enspiriting, and the most alluring invitation that I have received for a long time. Right gladly, indeed, will I make the journey to Worcester Park as soon as I feel fit for it. I have had to pay the penalty for my Omar[2]

[1] On 4 September 1894 Gissing made the following entry in his diary: "Went to Epsom and there at length found a house that pleases me—Eversley, Worple Road. Chalk and gravel. Decided to take house on yearly tenancy." (*Letters of George Gissing to His Family*, p. 339.)

[2] This dinner, held on November 20 at Frascati's, was the occasion of the first meeting between Gissing and Wells. The Omar Khayyám Club, a convivial organisation founded in 1894, held an annual country dinner. On the invitation of Clement Shorter, Gissing had attended the 1895 one, which was held at Burford Bridge Hotel for the convenience of George Meredith, the guest of honour. Among the speakers were Gissing and Hardy, who testified to the counsel and encouragement they had received from Meredith. Born on 22 November 1857, Gissing had published the following works: *Workers in the Dawn*, 1880; *The Unclassed*, 1884; *Isabel Clarendon*, 1886; *Demos*, 1886; *Thyrza*, 1887; *A Life's Morning*, 1888; *The Nether World*, 1889; *The Emancipated*, 1890; *New Grub Street*, 1891; *Born in Exile*, 1892; *Denzil Quarrier*, 1892; *The Odd Women*, 1893; *In the Year of Jubilee*, 1894; *The Paying Guest*, 1895; *Sleeping Fires*, 1895; *Eve's Ransom*, 1895. Nine years younger than Gissing, Wells had published the following romances and novels: *The Time Machine*, 1895; *The Wonderful Visit*, 1895; *The Island of Dr Moreau*, 1896; *The Wheels of Chance*, 1896.

dinner of the other evening in the shape of a violent cold,—nothing unusual, I am sorry to say. If this stops short of bronchitis or lung-congestion, I may get abroad in some ten days' time; but I long ago ceased to form any definite hopes that depended on the state of my body or mind.

Let me say, in the meantime, how thoroughly glad I am to hear from you, and how pleased to find (after having been much interested in your work), that personally you come so near my ideal of the brotherly man of letters. I see some reason to hope that your description of your new house does not too rigidly correspond with fact; for this is a time of year when defective roofs and so on play the devil with one's constitution. Mine was ruined in garrets and basements, some fifteen to twenty years ago.[1]

As for the—"pleasant home at Epsom," the less said

[1] Gissing here refers to the years 1877–82, when he lived in various lodgings in the vicinity of Islington and Tottenham Court Road and eked out an existence on the wages he received for tutoring—as low as four shillings for three hours—and the ten pounds a year accruing from a small inheritance. The shabbiness of his rooms was matched by the meagerness of his diet. Presumably on information from Gissing himself, Dr Henry Hick, in a letter of 7 February 1904 to Wells, itemised the daily menu of those hard years: "Breakfast—bread, dripping or butter, tea or coffee. Dinner—bread, bowl of soup made from a penny packet. Tea—bread, dripping or butter, tea or cocoa. Supper—bread, cheese, tea or cocoa. Occasionally a plate of beef at a cabman's shelter." It should be added that Austin Harrison declared that Gissing never suffered from poverty after 1882. ("George Gissing," *Nineteenth Century*, September 1906, pp. 453–463.)

about it the better.[1] One must have a local habitation, and here, somehow or other, I live; but I have never yet asked mortal to come and see me here—and probably never shall. For which, let my friends be grateful.

So, I will write again when I am able to leave home. But only on condition that you let me know it, with all emphasis, if I should propose to look in at a time which breaks your habits. If I did not myself live by rule and measure, I should do nothing at all, and I am so much afraid of wasting other men's time that it is a very rare thing indeed for me to call upon anyone.

Believe me,

Cordially yours,

GEORGE GISSING

[1] On 25 February 1891 Gissing married Edith Underwood, who has been unsympathetically and even unfairly treated by most writers on Gissing. Wells spoke of Gissing's "picking up a servant girl in Regent's Park one Sunday afternoon and marrying her." (*Experiment in Autobiography*, VIII, 3.) To the same effect Morley Roberts explained the marriage by attributing the following statement to Gissing: "I could stand it no longer, so I rushed out and spoke to the very first woman I came across." (*The Private Life of Henry Maitland*, p. 116.) In point of fact, five months intervened between the first meeting and the marriage of Gissing and Edith Underwood. Her ineptitude as a housekeeper was soon in evidence, and on the last day of 1892 Gissing noted in his diary that the year had been one of "domestic misery and discomfort." (*Letters of George Gissing to His Family*, p. 331.)

2

WELLS TO GISSING

Heatherlea, Worcester Park, Surrey

[30 *November* 1896]

MY DEAR GISSING, (The Beast grows familiar) I want to see you now much more than I did, and I hope this clear dry weather will do its duty by your cold. And as for bronchitis and so forth, if you want to meet a man of extraordinary gifts in that way, you cannot do better than meet me. You could not possibly waste my time, but it will be wiser all the same to warn me of your advent lest you find me away on some fool's business or other. Besides walking it is possible to reach this place by passenger train to Worcester Park.[1]

Take care of yourself, there's a good chap! because now I've written you so impudently—after a struggle with my natural shyness if you will believe me—and you've answered so kindly, I've a sort of feeling that this should have happened before.

Yours ever

H. G. WELLS

[1] At this point in the letter Wells drew a map showing the way from the station to Heatherlea.

3

WELLS TO GISSING

Heatherlea, Worcester Park, Surrey

[*c.* 6 *December* 1896]

My dear Gissing, On Wednesday next I am going to the *N. Vagabonds* dinner[1] with my wife. I shall have to begin cleaning and overhauling myself by 5.10. So if you want a real interminable gossip (as I do) it isn't long enough. But I shall be in after two and waiting for you. Are you thinking of that dinner at all? If so would you care to come in with us?

Yours ever
H. G. W.

4

GISSING TO WELLS

8 *December* 1896 *Eversley, Worple Road, Epsom*

My dear Wells, I was unlucky. My 2.40 train would probably not enable me to reach you till after 3—and, as

[1] The New Vagabonds Club held a dinner on 10 December 1896 at which Wells was the guest of honour. He made it the subject of a "picshua" which includes drawings of Jerome K. Jerome, Sidney Low, Douglas Sladen, and Kenneth Grahame. (*Experiment in Autobiography*, VIII, 3.)

you say, there would be no time. I know how disagreeable it is to have to calculate one's minutes in making ready for dinners. That is one reason why I dread and shun such things as much as possible. My name, bythebye, is among the New Vagabonds by mistake. I was elected without having been told anything about it, and, at the risk of giving offence (heaven knows I meant none) had to beg to be let off. The Omar is the only club I belong to, of any kind, and I simply dare not go in for more conviviality. The fact is, I enjoy it too much, and could easily become a mere haunter of taverns.[1]

It shall be the Wednesday of next week—if this will suit you. If not, I can easily come at another time. Don't trouble yourself to write; you are a busy man, and will come to loathe my name and address. I shall know it is all right if I don't hear.

What a blessed flow of vitality in your *Wheels of Chance*![2] And you are so *various*.

Always yours,
GEORGE GISSING

[1] At first glance this statement may seem to be out of character, but Wells declared that Gissing "craved to laugh, jest, enjoy, stride along against the wind, shout, 'quaff mighty flagons.'" (*Experiment in Autobiography*, VIII, 3.) Similarly Brian Ború Dunne, who met Gissing in Italy in 1898, wrote in a letter of 21 January 1933 to Wells, "I look upon Gissing as one of the most cheerful, luxury-loving, witty people I have ever met."

[2] *The Wheels of Chance* is a humorous, whimsical story about the cycling holiday of a draper's assistant. In remarking on Wells's variety Gissing was probably referring to *The Island of Dr*

5

GISSING TO WELLS

c/o H. Hick, Esq., New Romney, Kent

14 *February* 1897

MY DEAR WELLS, Could you manage to dine with me, at 7, on Tuesday evening,—the place Previtali's? I should be very glad. On that day I am coming up to town to see a scoundrel specialist[1] in diseases of the lungs, who is as likely as not to upset all my plans of life. But don't be afraid of my company; you shall hear no pathology.

There will be with me at Previtali's an old schoolfellow of mine, a country surgeon, in whose house I am staying at present.[2] He would think it very delightful to meet you.

Moreau, also published in 1896. The satire and the gruesome details in this work were too relentless and horrible for most of the reviewers.

[1] Dr Philip Henry Pye-Smith advised a warm climate, and Gissing spent three months (February–April) at Budleigh Salterton, Devon, a resort which he knew from his residence in Exeter (1891–93).

[2] A domestic crisis had driven Gissing from home. Distraught and ill, he went to Dr Henry Hick. The two had become acquainted in childhood when Gissing's father bought a chemist's shop in Wakefield, Yorkshire, from Hick's father. The boys were schoolmates but did not renew their friendship until 1894. Hick became a friend, as well as doctor, to Wells, with whom he corresponded for more than thirty years.

If you can post reply early on Monday (to-morrow) I shall get it before leaving here the next morning.

Heartily yours,

GEORGE GISSING

6

WELLS TO GISSING

Heatherlea, Worcester Park, Surrey

Bank Holiday [16 *April* 1897]

MY DEAR GISSING, On Wednesday at latest Madame and I will DV start for Petersfield in Hampshire—on our way to you. We shall reach Budleigh Salterton on Monday or Tuesday evening so that rooms might be taken for us (if you have not repented of your promise) for Monday onward. I have just been reading *The Whirlpool*[1]—but I am not going to waste conversation in letters. I had set my heart on reviewing the book for the *Saturday*. And so had Harold Frederic.[2] And as he was the more alert he bagged it. Damn him!

I had a letter from Hick and he tells me you are very much better.

Madame says I have given no indication of the sort of

[1] *The Whirlpool*, Gissing's seventeenth novel, was published in May.

[2] Frederic (1856–98), American journalist and novelist, who went to England in 1884 as correspondent of the *New York Times*. See Letters 55, 57, and 58.

rooms we want. But any sort will do, provided they are clean and the people of the house not so genteel as to shame two dirty cyclists.—one bed room and one sitting room is the technical thing she says. Go on and say that.

Our warmest regards.

Yours ever

H. G. WELLS

A Frenchman named Davray[1] who was here on Saturday came hither from George Meredith, who had *The Whirlpool* in hand and expounded it to him. Meredith was all for praise.

7

WELLS TO GISSING

18 *May* 1897 *Dartmouth*

HONOURED SIR, We beg to report our personal safety. We were unable to land at Teignmouth (Providential interposition) and went on to Torcross.[2] We landed there in surf and found the place delightful. Slate rocks, grey, green, blue silver changing colour like the sea and sky, quartz veins, sea pinks, yellow wallflowers, yellow

[1] Henry D. Davray (1873–1944) was for many years in charge of the section on foreign literature in the *Mercure de France*. He translated several of Wells's books into French, the first of them *The War of the Worlds* (1900).

[2] In the margin Wells wrote: "Strongly advise you to go to Torcross it's ripping."

lichens, white campions. Magnificent walk of 8 miles (eight miles)—very hot, very dusty but very magnificent —hither. A glittering morning today. We watched you on the beach until you were this size[1] and then you turned about and went slowly townward.

Our best wishes

Yours ever

H. G.

8

WELLS TO GISSING

21 *May* 1897 *Tavistock*

MY DEAR GISSING, This records the continued success of the Journey. The Expedition left Dartmouth on Wednesday afternoon in a steamboat for Totnes trotted through that charming place in an hour (1 hour) seeing a castle (with a superb view) and several gates. Thence by train to Buckfastleigh (night). The next day rain hot the expedition (damp hot and cheerful) trudged to Holme and Sharp Tor (night) Yesterday gorgeous and the Dart from Holme Chase to Dartmeet magnificent. Train from Princetown hither. The Expedition is in excellent health and sends the warmest regards.

Yours ever

H. G.

[1] Here Wells drew a dot enclosed in a circle.

9

GISSING TO WELLS

22 May 1897 *Budleigh Salterton*

MY DEAR WELLS, I cannot hit you with a letter on your route, but it seems such ingratitude to keep silence whilst you are delighting me with these reports, that I must address to Heatherlea, for your reading when you arrive. Great heavens! what weather you have had. East wind, to be sure, but probably you did not mind that, with such a sky. Of course I have thought of you ceaselessly, rejoicing as each day broke with renewed glory. This is the kind of thing that sends a man back to work with exultant spirits.

Only last night (Friday) did I receive *Black and White*.[1] I shall put the number carefully away, and hope (daringly enough) that ten years hence I may light upon it, and that we three may then revive in some quiet hour of gossip the time when it appeared. The "prose fancy" is right daintily done; with a very light hand, where lightness of hand was everything. Only one word in it could I wish changed; but as that word reminds me of a brutal remark I once made to you, I shall not mention it. The English is very good and most pleasantly unaffected.

[1] Catherine Wells's "My Grandfather's Shirt-Studs," which appeared in *Black and White* (8 May 1897), is a humourous sketch with an overtone of pathos.

You have probably seen the notice of your book in the *Chronicle*.[1] Not bad—though of course justice is not done to the last story. Ah, but you are an enviable man! With your gusto for work, your happiness, your capabilities, what may you not do!

I draw near to the end of the legible section of Cassiodorus.[2] One bit was so curiously interesting (reproving the inhabitants of Bruttium for abandoning their cities and going to live in rural places) that I had half a mind to translate the whole page for you. But you have had enough of the old pedant.

My kindest regards to Mrs Wells.

Yours ever,

GEORGE GISSING

[1] The *Daily Chronicle* (20 May 1897) lavished praise upon *The Plattner Story and Others*, declaring that Wells was the greatest living master of the Almost Incredible. But the reviewer criticised the last story, "A Slip under the Microscope," for raising a nice question of ethics and answering it in the wrong way—"by saying that, having told a lie, one should stick to it." Actually the point of the story, which deals with an almost accidental case of cheating in an examination, is that there is no ready answer to so simple a problem as this: it involves social rank, parental influence, diet, love, and political views.

[2] Gissing found in Cassiodorus's *Variae* the germinal idea for *Veranilda.* Wells, who with his wife spent some time in Budleigh Salterton near Gissing, recalled that he had "two or three great Latin tomes in which he read and dreamt . . . he was annotating the works of Cassiodorus." (*Monthly Review*, August 1904, p. 168.) The diary shows that in June Gissing was systematically studying Manso's *Geschichte des ostgothischen Reiches in Italien*, Burn's *Rome and the Campagna*, and similar books.

I rejoice to see that Longmans promise Hudson's new Book—*Birds in London.*[1]

10

GISSING TO WELLS

23 *June* 1897 *Epsom*

MY DEAR WELLS, You know not how difficult it is for me to get an hour or two of leisure. Since returning,[2] I have seen no one but the doctor. But listen. On Sat. July 10, I have to go to the Omar dinner at Marlowe.[3] There, perforce, I shall stay overnight, and on the Sunday morning I shall look in upon good old Hudson, at Westbourne Park—whom I have not seen for a year. Now there is a train which reaches Worcester Park at 2.5, and, if I do not hear that this will disarrange you, I shall give myself the

[1] In his diary and letters Gissing frequently mentions W. H. Hudson (1841–1922), always with sympathy and affection. The two men were brought together by Morley Roberts some time before 1884.

[2] Gissing was persuaded to return to Epsom for the summer by Miss Clara Collet and Miss Eliza Orme, who hoped to resolve the domestic discord. Miss Collet (1860–1948), an employee of the Board of Trade, admired Gissing's novels, and made them the subject of a lecture to the London Ethical Society in 1892. For Miss Orme see Letter 19.

[3] On July 10 Gissing noted in his diary that Barrie, a new member of the club, did not attend the dinner. His absence must have been a disappointment to Gissing, for on June 1 he had received from Barrie an enthusiastic letter about *The Whirlpool.*

pleasure of seeing you then—you will have finished luncheon.

I wish you a fine day for Spithead; it will be glorious on the sea.[1]

Remembrances to Mrs Wells and to Mrs Robbins.[2]

Yours always, my dear boy,

GEORGE GISSING

It goes without saying that you bid me avaunt if you have another plan for that day. Silence will mean agreement.[3]

II

GISSING TO WELLS

7 *August* 1897 *Castle Bolton, Leyburn, Yorkshire* [4]

MY DEAR WELLS, You must have suffered greatly at Worcester Park from the heat of this last week. Even

[1] The naval review at Spithead, June 26, was one of the notable events of Queen Victoria's Diamond Jubilee. Ships of all nations, extending for thirty miles, made a spectacle which was ecstatically reported in the Press. The day did prove to be a fine one. The Jubilee is the subject of *The Private Papers of Henry Ryecroft*, "Summer," XX.

[2] The mother of Mrs Wells.

[3] Gissing did in fact spend the afternoon and evening with the Wellses.

[4] Ironically this Wensleydale setting for Gissing's vain attempt to achieve domestic harmony was to figure prominently in *The Crown of Life*, the novel in which he expressed his love for Gabrielle Fleury.

here, high on the hills, it was at times all but intolerable. I took refuge in a lovely glen, where, between great firs and pines, a "beck" rushes over limestone boulders down to the river Ure,—and there, bythebye, I read your *Contemporary* article.[1]

Admirably written, this same article; I wish I had half the critical ability which you show throughout. Of course I read with peculiar interest, and at times with peculiar feeling; but the sum of it all is that I believe you have seen justly and spoken as it behoved you to do. I have always been drearily conscious of the immaturity discoverable in all my work; the worst of it is, I cannot hope with you that I shall make much more progress. I lack the vital energy that would justify such a hope; what I have is frittered away in mean squabbling and sordid cares.—But you know all about that.

Let me say a word or two on certain details of your paper.

In Rolfe I wished to present a man whose character developed with unusual slowness, and who would probably never have developed at all, after a certain stage, but for the change wrought in his views and sentiments by the fact of his becoming a father. The early passage of his talk which you quote (about children) is meant to contrast strongly with his way of thinking and speaking

[1] "The Novels of Mr George Gissing," *Contemporary Review* (August 1897). Reprinted in the present volume as Appendix C, pp. 242–259.

in the latter part of the book. As a bachelor, he was largely an egoist, and took the egoistic tone of a certain world. Later he is ripe in that experience which kills the cruder egoism. That he *does* nothing is natural in the man—"Whirlpool" influences embarrass any efficiency there might have been in him. Though the most likely man in my circle of characters (excluding Morton) to be a profitable citizen, that hope is spoilt by his surroundings. "The Whirlpool," you say, "should be devouring him." It *has* devoured only too much of him, as of many another such fellow.

In that last talk with Morton, I never meant to suggest that Rolfe tended to the "Barrack-room" view of life. In all he says, he is simply expressing his hopeless recognition of facts which fill him with disgust. Thus and thus—says he—is the world going; no refusing to see it; it stares us in the eyes; but what a course for things to take!—He talks with a little throwing-up of the arm, and in a voice of quiet sarcasm. Go ahead! I sit by and watch, and wonder what'll be the end of it all.

Now this, I rather think, is my own habit of mind of late years. I have come to recognize a course of things which formerly I could not—or would not—perceive; and I do it with just that tossing of arm and head—involuntary, of course. I have a conviction that all I love and believe in is going to the devil; at the same time, I try to watch with interest this process of destruction, admiring any bit of sapper-work that is well done.

You say that *The Whirlpool* amounts "very nearly to a flat contradiction of the ideals of the immature *Emancipated*." Why then, it is plain to me that *The Emancipated* must be even more immature, more ineffectively written, than I thought. For, in my mind, the ideals of one book are precisely those of the other. The title of *The Emancipated* is ironical. In Mallard and his wife, at the end, I wanted to show two people who had settled down to a wholesome, unpretending life of work and duties; having got rid of superstitions (old and new), but too old and too wise to make any fuss about it.

Come, come—I doubt if you will read all this. Among other old fashions, I am rather given to the writing of long letters; which you, I fancy, abhor. But remember, I beg, that I have hitherto had but one serious correspondent (old Bertz).[1] Don't imagine me pouring out

[1] Eduard Bertz, a socialist refugee from Bismarck's Germany, inserted an advertisement in a London paper expressing a desire to meet an Englishman who enjoyed scholarly conversation. Gissing answered, and the two met in early January 1879. Bertz was partially responsible for Gissing's temporary interest in socialism, and his experience as a teacher in a girl's school near Brighton supplied Gissing with some episodes in *The Unclassed*. In 1881 Bertz joined the co-operative colony in Tennessee inspired by Thomas Hughes, but returned disillusioned two years later. Gissing helped him secure a publisher for a boy's story, the proceeds from which enabled him to return to Germany. There he entered literary journalism and the book trade, and made every effort to win German readers for Gissing. The two men corresponded regularly through the years, and Bertz appeared in *The Private Papers of Henry Ryecroft*, "Autumn," VII. (Arthur C. Young, "George Gissing's Friendship with Eduard Bertz," *Nineteenth-Century Fiction*, December 1958, pp. 227–237.)

daily at this length and on such matters. You need never trouble to answer. I know you will take it all good-naturedly, prose as I may, and that's enough.

The life here shows little trace of *vortical* influence. In this hamlet there is no shop, no inn, no post office. We have three rooms in a little cottage, looking across Wensleydale to a great green hill, wooded and craggy. At night the air murmurs with the music of a waterfall two miles away; and there is crying of owls—a sound peculiarly delightful to me.

When you send me a line (and I know you will before the end of August) tell me if your article gave occasion to any journalistic remark worth repeating.

The boy Walter[1] is enjoying himself. He remembers you well.

My very kind regards to your wife and Mrs Robbins, and believe me

Always heartily yours,

GEORGE GISSING

[1] Gissing's elder son, then aged five.

12

WELLS TO GISSING

Heatherlea, Worcester Park, Surrey[1]

[*c.* 10 *August* 1897]

My dear Gissing, I've had a sort of nervous period since that article appeared and your letter was a very welcome termination thereunto. The stuff was criticism of a sort, and by no means an appreciation, which from me would have been a little impertinent, quite graceless and (as some people know I know you personally) of no benefit to either of us. I think I see your point on Rolfe and Morton—but I always give myself the benefit of a delay before I admit an error. There's a trickle of little mentions like the enclosed—one in *Daily Chronicle* of a brief but friendly sort.[2] Where there is more than mention there is misconception (naturally) as in the *Speaker*.[3] I envy you moorland. We are very hot and close here, and I have been very much worried by a commission for two short stories and an inability to get up to the mark with them—a consequent disorganization—nerves wrong—sleeplessness, swearing, weeping. I've resigned myself to do the things this morning rather than do them badly and

[1] In the upper margin Wells wrote: "Have you heard from Hick—brevity remarkable."

[2] Unidentified.

[3] Unidentified.

am resuming my normal state of mind.[1] Funny beasts we are! Give Walter our warmest regards.

Yours ever

H. G.

13

GISSING TO WELLS

11 *August* 1897 *Castle Bolton, Leyburn, Yorkshire*

MY DEAR WELLS, You are a facetious man and on first reading your letter this morning I felt a doubt whether I was to take you literally. I think, however, that you really mean what you say, and I reply with all gravity.

The grounds of Bullen's objections are clear to me.[2] He sees things from the point of view of journalists and

[1] During the summer of 1897 Wells wrote these stories: "The Crystal Egg," "Story of the Stone Age," and "The Star." They were published in the *New Review*, the *Idler*, and the *Graphic*.

[2] After editing Marlowe, Campion, and other Elizabethans, A. H. Bullen (1857–1920) entered publishing in 1891. His handling of *Certain Personal Matters*, a collection of Wells's journalistic pieces, caused some clashes of opinion. When Bullen recommended the omission of one paper, "On Schooling and the Phases of Mr Sandstone," Wells insisted that it be placed first in the book. Bullen agreed to restore it, but reduced it to seventh place and called attention to a passage of ungainly humour in it. Wells promptly asked that an illustration of his own design be included with a statement to that effect on the title-page. When Bullen replied that this would be more appropriate for a sixpenny jest-book than for a six-shilling volume of essays, Wells advised a price of 3s. 6d. and still insisted on the title-page. Bullen suggested that the matter be arbitrated by Gissing, who, as the publisher anticipated, decided in his favour.

public. I myself see a decided danger in your suggestion; depend upon it, certain reviewers would pounce upon this jest and make a detrimental use of it. Many readers, too, would resent it (you know the literal dogs) as a deliberate misrepresentation. The fact of the matter is,—permit me to say,—that your book will be altogether too good for this kind of thing. I have been reading the pages you enclose, and they give one a decided appetite for more. Mind—I do not say that the *drawing* is out of place; indeed I think it very amusing. I only mean that the joke on the title-page would be too emphatic—out of proportion,—and most certainly you would have many an occasion to bite your lips in wrath at things said and printed about it.

Between ourselves, Bullen is a trifle positive in his judgments and modes of expression; an excellent fellow, for all that, and I should be grieved beyond measure if you came to blows on the matter of a title-page. Calm yourself, I beg, and try to believe that there *is* a valid objection from the commercial point of view—indeed, as I have said, from another as well. Your book will be delightful; do not give the least occasion for unfriendly remark upon it.

Many thanks for the newspaper cuttings, which I return. I heartily agree with the spirit in which you approached and executed that task; certainly no other was possible under the circumstances.

Yours ever, my dear H. G.,

George Gissing

14

GISSING TO WELLS

26 *August* 1897 *Eversley, Worple Road, Epsom*

MY DEAR H. G., Now do be careful! I chanced to meet Pinker[1] at Waterloo to-day, and he confirms my suspicion that you have been working too long and too hard. Avast—heaving—as soon as possible. I loathe the thought of your falling ill.

May I beg you to transfer the enclosed to the said Pinker—whose address I know not and of whose initials I am equally ignorant. It is about a business matter, of which Pinker will perchance speak to you some day.[2]

I shall have to see you in a week or so. Will write again.

Kind regards, as always, to your household.

Yours ever,

GEORGE GISSING

[1] James B. Pinker (1863–1922) resigned as editor of *Pearson's Magazine* at the close of 1895 and set up as a literary agent. In a letter of 13 January 1896 Pinker informed Wells of his venture and was shortly placing some of Wells's work in various periodicals.

[2] Apparently Gissing asked Pinker to sell the American rights of *Human Odds and Ends*, but nothing came of the attempt. (Gordan, *George Gissing*, p. 33.)

15

GISSING TO WELLS

5 *September* 1897 *Eversley*, *Worple Road*, *Epsom*

MY DEAR WELLS, There was a half promise, made at Budleigh, that you and your wife would eat with me at the Criterion some day. (You know the miserable impossibility of my ever entertaining friends at home.) Now, in a fortnight or so I am leaving England for six months, and of course we must talk together before I go.[1] Do you think, then, that we could arrange for a luncheon at the Criterion on Sat. Sept. 11? You know how much I should enjoy it. Could you spare the time—and would Mrs Wells care to come? If so, please let me have a line before then. I go into Hampshire for a day or two on Wednesday.

I hope Brighton has done you good. I shall have much to tell you.[2]

[1] On September 17 Gissing parted from his wife, almost exactly seven years from the date of their first meeting.

[2] Half the page is cut away, and Gissing's signature is missing. However, *Gissing*, in his hand, stands above the date.

16

GISSING TO WELLS

21 *September* 1897 *Wakefield*

MY DEAR WELLS, After packing the 2 vols. of Cassiodorus, I hesitated.[1] It was evident that the cost of the carriage to Italy would be nearly the price of the book. I decided that I must re-read the old chap in a library at Rome; it will do me no harm.

The rush and uproar and labour of these last few days have been terrific.[2] Never mind; one more chapter of life is closed—one more step towards the happy Finis.

Of course you will hear from me. Do not neglect to let me hear of *anything* that affects you—even a trifle will have its interest out yonder. The foreign post-cards are of good size.

And come, and if come you can. News of your decision would make me shout for joy.[3]

[1] S. V. Gapp, in *George Gissing Classicist* (1936), pondered the question as to whether Gissing carried these bulky volumes on his Italian journey. In the *Monthly Review* (August 1904) Wells vividly recalled how one day at Lulworth Cove Gissing described his longing to go to Italy and drew from his pocket-book some mementoes of his earlier trip. Among them was a ticket to the reading-room of the Vatican library.

[2] As a preliminary to the trip to Italy Gissing spent September 17–21 visiting his mother, sisters, and son in Yorkshire.

[3] Wells remembered that at an Omar Khayyán dinner Gissing urged him to visit Rome. That dinner may have been the one held at Marlow on July 10. See Letter 5.

Good-bye to you all. I measure my language in saying, that, after my little boys, there are no people in England of whom I shall think more frequently.

Eat well, and be moderate with the bicycle. Thereto, remember me always as

Very truly your friend,
GEORGE GISSING

17

GISSING TO MRS WELLS

3 *October* 1897 *Via delle Belle Arti, 18, 3°. piano, Siena*

DEAR MRS WELLS, Doubtless H. G. received my post-card[1] from Milan. Heavens! how the white marble of the Duomo gleamed against the sky that morning! On the wearisome journey from there to Siena of course I caught a cold; but I am vigorously shaking it off.[2] Last week the weather was simply tropical; the people here called it unusual; all but impossible to cross a broad space of sunshine. Now it is cloudy and cool, and at this

[1] The card is missing.

[2] Gissing left London on September 22 and, by way of Basle, arrived in Milan the following evening. On September 25 he went to Siena and two days later was comfortably settled and taking up his work. He was too sanguine about the cold: it was in Siena that he noticed for the first time the stain of blood on his handkerchief. (Gordan, *George Gissing*, p. 43.)

height (1000 ft.) one feels the pleasantness of an English summer.

Switzerland was green and grand, but shadowed already by the coming winter. The mountain torrents, swollen by melting of early snow, came down every few miles in leaps of hundreds of feet—a glorious sight. That S. Gotthard line is tremendous; in places it frightens one.

I passed one night here at a hotel, then looked about for a private lodging, and with remarkable success. Of course I have only one room, but I take my meals with the family; excellent middle-class people, who improve my Italian from day to day, knowing no language but their own. My room is spacious, with two windows, which look across a hollow of houses to the Cathedral on its hill-top. The ceiling is elaborately painted, with a design in which ultramarine predominates; the floor, of course uncarpeted, is of red tiles; the walls, which seem to be papered, are in reality painted (stencil, no doubt,) on plaster, with another design in ultramarine. The framed pictures are: Prince of Naples, S. Catherine, S. Mary.

I eat thus: Breakfast: coffee, bread and butter. Lunch: soup, meat, vegetables, cheese, fruit, pint of wine. Dinner: same as lunch, with an extra course, and salad. And now, what do you think I pay for *board and lodging*? Well, not quite £4 a month! I am bound to admit that, considering the superior character of the house, this is cheap even for Italy.

But think what this cheapness of everything must be to the natives. Wine, for instance. I see that the best quality sells for c5 a litre, and the last for c2½.

An old, old place. One lives in the middle ages, with frequent reminders of a yet older time. From the street of S. Mark I turn into the Street of Diana—and so on. The houses are very high, so as to exclude the terrible sun from the narrow ways—which, bythebye, have no side-walks. Ordinary carts are drawn by splendid white oxen, with grand horns—the very oxen of Virgil and Homer.

Last Sunday there was a great pilgrimage to the shrine of S. Catherine, and her *head* was exhibited, above the altar in the chapel.[1] Yes, her actual head; and in a skilful arrangement of candles it made a strange impression; I looked at it with profound reverence—and a lump in the throat. (a photograph I bought is rather horrible.)

She lived in a street close by here; her house has been ever since an oratory. Her father was a dyer, and, as I am only too well aware with the wind in a certain quarter,

[1] The sympathetic response to the shrine of St Catherine is interesting in view of Wells's assertion that Gissing thought Christianity "a deplorable disaster" and felt such an antipathy for it that he left the Wellses to see the Vatican and St Peter's by themselves when they came to Rome. (*Experiment in Autobiography*, VIII, 3.) Brian Ború Dunne, for whom see Letter 32, suggests that Gissing did not escort the Wellses for these reasons: (1) they did not need a guide; (2) Gissing was "very busy with his research work in a Roman library"; (3) Gissing was very sensitive about his appearance and "may have been short on white shirts." (From a letter of 18 February 1959 to the editor.)

dyers still inhabit that street—still, after 500 years, unlike the majority of saints, she is a very human and loveable creature; pray read about her, if you forget her life. I often turn into the church of San Domenico, where she worshipped, and where are preserved certain marble steps on which she trod.

To-day I have had a country walk. From hills at a little distance one looks back on Siena, surrounded with its walls and gates—a true mediaeval stronghold. All the purpose served by the walls and gates at present is to exact dues from the peasantry as they come or go with articles of food, etc.

The flora of the wayside is practically English. Very strange, amid grapes, olives and figs, to see hedges of bramble overgrown with traveller's joy, flowering dogwood, the hawkweeds, mints, and so on.—Of course all this changes in the far south. Indeed, north and south Italy are two different countries. Much more comfortable here, but you cannot think how I long for Calabria.

Does one *like* Italy? The fact is, I always feel it is a terrible country; its unspeakable beauty is inseparable from the darkest thoughts; go where you may, you see the traces of blood and tears. To be sure, this will apply to the whole world; but here one *remembers* so much more than in other countries. Age after age of strife and tyranny, of vast calamities, of unimaginable suffering in the palace and the hut. You feel something pitiless in the blue sky that has looked so tranquilly on all this. And the people—you see centuries of oppression in their faces, hear it in their voice. Yes, yes, one likes Italy; but in a very special sense of the word.

I enclose for you a leaf of olive which I picked by the roadside this morning. Think of all it means—a leaf of the olive of Italy!

Well, you can read this letter at two sittings.—I have made a good beginning with my Dickens, and long to have done it, for of course it is an alien subject.[1]

San Domenico is ringing mid-day, and here comes the daughter of the house knocking at my door—"Signore, la tavola!" To which I reply, "Eccomi, Signorina!"—and go to lunch.

After saying, what you know, that I remember with much kindness all at Heatherlea, and desire to be remembered by them.

Always sincerely yours,
GEORGE GISSING

[1] This is an interesting statement in view of Gissing's reputation as a Dickensian. The fact that an old friend from Owens College days, J. H. Rose, commissioned the book for the Victorian Era Series suggests that Gissing's interest in Dickens was of long standing. But writing to Edward Clodd on 1 September 1898 Gissing declared, "I should *like* to try my hand at Thackeray, who, be it said between us, appeals to me much more strongly than Dickens." (Clodd, *Memories*, p. 170.) Actually while Gissing was at Budleigh Salterton he began his preparation for the book on Dickens by reading widely in the novels.

18

GISSING TO WELLS [postcard]

16 *October* 1897 *Via Belle Arti, 18, Siena*

I am delighted to receive your book.[1] I have glanced through it and joyfully anticipate the reading. Your letter also came safely. I fag on at the Dickens book, of which, heaven be thanked, nearly half is done.[2] Weather again very warm; a south wind which does not leave one much superfluous energy.—A great deal in Italian papers about the great strike.[3] No malicious comments; much good feeling towards England.—Very bad reports from Sicily; bad harvest, peasants dying of hunger by road-sides. You read about the riot in Rome?[4] It would be amusing if my

[1] *The Invisible Man*, published in September 1897.

[2] Writing to his brother on October 12 Gissing reported that by working from nine to twelve and two to six he was writing two thousand words a day. He expressed satisfaction at the quality of the work though he found it slower than fiction. (*Letters of George Gissing to His Family*, p. 354.)

[3] The strike was a bitter contest over the eight-hour day between the 90,000 members of the Amalgamated Society of Engineers and their employers. The latter were so relentless in their refusal to mediate that the British people and the press sympathised with the workers. The strike lasted from July 1897 until January 1898, when the engineers capitulated.

[4] Italy was suffering from her persistent problems—poverty and taxation. A change in the taxes caused a large crowd to gather in the Piazza Navona. In dispersing it the infantry killed one man and wounded several, causing much indignation in Rome.

stay here were enlivened by a revolution—not impossible.

Kindest remembrances to you all.

G. G.

19

GISSING TO WELLS [postcard]

5 *November* 1897 *Siena*

Hearty thanks for the *Nat. Review*.[1] I perceive that it was written 3 or 4 years ago, and no effort made to bring it up to date—rather a discouraging affair altogether.

Well, heaven be praised, my book is just done,[2] and on Monday I go to Rome. A stay there of two days, to present a letter of introduction; then on to Naples, where I must stay to get what help I can, for Calabria, from Marion Crawford.[3] A day or two only, I hope. Then begins the real travel—how I look forward to it.—I have

[1] The *National Review* for October 1897 published a respectful appraisal of Gissing's novels by Frederick Dolman, who stated that their persistent theme was "impatience with the present competitive phase of society, with its mad striving for wealth on the one side and its painful struggle for subsistence on the other." Dolman passed over the later novels with the comment that they dealt with sexual relations rather than the problem of society.

[2] On the following day Gissing sent the manuscript of *Charles Dickens: A Critical Study* to his agent, William Morris Colles, for whom see Letter 33.

[3] The American novelist Francis Marion Crawford (1854–1909) lived in Sorrento from 1885 until his death.

seen very little of Siena—regular 7 hours' work a day, amid serious difficulties. My landlady's husband has died, and we have changed to another house. Imagine me grappling with such circumstances. But it has given me a valuable glimpse of intimate life.

Your book has delighted me of evenings.[1] Much of it is excellent, and all good—thoroughly your own. You owe allegiance to no man.

Of course you shall hear from the land of the sun. First stoppage after Rome will be Monte Cassino—which I forgot to mention.

Very hearty remembrances to you all. Are you well? I do hope so. Ask Mrs Wells to keep a very grave eye upon you.

Yours always,

G. G.

The only safe address, till you hear again, is *Poste restante*, *Napoli*. They will forward letters to me.

20

GISSING TO WELLS [postcard]

13 *November* 1897 *Naples*

I am starting on my journey. The book was finished in Siena, and I have heard of its safe receipt.[2] The British

[1] *The Invisible Man.*

[2] In December Colles sent Gissing a typescript of the study of Dickens for correction.

Consul here has given me letters to a lot of useful people in Calabria.[1] If you can find time, how it will delight me to hear from you. Please address thus:

Poste restante,
Catanzaro.
Calabria Ulteriore, Italy

Catanzaro is not far from Squillace; you will perhaps find it on the map. I hope to be there in 3 or 4 weeks' time, and to find a heap of letters.[2] || Vesuvius a fine sight after dark; about a mile of lava glows red from a smoke crater at the foot of the cone. How I am glorying in Naples—it is my third visit.[3] The most interesting town (modern interest) in the world! || Kindest remembrances to you all. Drink a bottle of wine for me on Nov. 22, my 40th birthday. I shall be among the mountains, or by the Ionian Sea. || Heavens! what talk we will have, some day.

Ever yours,
G. G.

[1] Among these was a letter to Signor Pasquale Gricelli, who figures interestingly in *By the Ionian Sea.*

[2] Twenty-three letters awaited him at Catanzaro.

[3] Gissing had spent November 1888 in Naples. The following year, in a mood of despondency and frustration, he again went to the continent, as far as Athens, and on his return journey stayed some weeks (December 1889–January 1890) in Naples. In *By the Ionian Sea* Gissing declared that he found Naples dull compared with what it was on his previous visits.

21

GISSING TO WELLS [postcard]

20 *November* 1897 *Taranto*

Thus far I have carried out my plans.[1] The journey across the mountains from Paola was wonderful, and Cosenza very interesting. Though it involved covering the same route twice, I have come from Cosenza to Taranto to get the advice of the Director of the Museum here, before I stop at Sybaris, Croton and the other coast places. Weather bad for Italy; sky always heavily clouded. But very warm. Taranto—wonderful place for fish; I have eaten the most extraordinary marine creatures.

It will disappoint me much if I do not find a line from you at Catanzaro, some 10 days hence. I hope all is well at Heatherlea. Yours

G. G.

[1] Gissing left Naples on November 16 and reached Paola the following morning. He spent the night at Cosenza and proceeded to Taranto where he remained until the morning of November 24. During his stay he wrote "At the Grave of Alaric", an article reprinted in *Selections from the Works of George Gissing*, pp. 238–244. He later made the grave of Alaric the subject of the interesting third chapter of *By the Ionian Sea*.

22

GISSING TO WELLS [postcard]

7 *December* 1897 [*Catanzaro*]

Delighted to receive your *sign-manual*, here at Catanzaro.[1] After receipt of this, please address

Poste restante,
Roma.

I go from here to Squillace, thence to Reggio, and thence to the dear old City, where I shall be at home once more.

Rather cold here among these mountains. Wonderful place this; how I wish you could be here![2] I have been ill in bed for six days, at Cotrone—a dire experience.[3] Cotrone is *Croton*—quantum mutata!

Kindest remembrances to all.

G. G.

[1] Gissing arrived in Catanzaro at six o'clock on the night of December 6 and remained until December 10.

[2] Gissing had supposed that he would find Catanzaro an uninteresting place because he "could attach to it no classic memory." But Chapters XII–XIII of *By the Ionian Sea* testify to his enjoyment of it and also prove that he was not simply an antiquarian.

[3] Gissing's diary for December 1, 2, 4, and 5 describes his illness, which is also recounted very interestingly in Chapters VII–X of *By the Ionian Sea.*

23

GISSING TO WELLS [postcard]

15 *December* 1897 [*Monte Cassino*]

I write to you from *Monte Cassino*, after passing the night in the great Monastery of S. Benedict.[1] The weather is bad (no sun!)—but scenery glorious beyond description. Very impressive, the night in the monastery, on the top of a mountain some 1500 ft. high. Snow on the Apennines. To-night I return to Rome.—What a talk we will have one of these days!

G. G.

24

GISSING TO WELLS [postcard]

20 *December* 1897 *Via del Boschetto*, 41 *A*, *Roma*[2]

All good wishes for Xmas and New Year! Dining at a restaurant this evening, I picked up a Roman newspaper, in which your Martian book[3] is noticed. In the joy of my

[1] Leaving Catanzaro on the morning of December 10 Gissing saw the site of the monastery of Cassiodorus at Squillace, and, by way of Reggio and Naples, he arrived in Monte Cassino on December 14. His visit to the monastery there was partly motivated by a desire to work up the background for *Veranilda*.

[2] Gissing arrived in Rome on the evening of December 15.

[3] *The War of the Worlds* (1898) was serialised in *Pearson's Magazine* (April–December 1897).

heart, I drank 3 great bottles of wine, and was carried home in a sad state.—Seriously, it is a great thing to be written and read in Rome.

Newspaper posted to-day.

G. G.

25

WELLS TO GISSING

Heatherlea, Worcester Park, Surrey

[*c.* 1 *January* 1898]

MY DEAR GISSING, Want of system and industry are, I must confess, in part answerable for the silence, but I had hoped with the new year to get things sufficiently fixed up to tell positively that we could come to Italy. But as you may have heard before *Ars longa, vita brevis*—nothing is finished and nothing settled. I do still hope. But only dogged industry will finish these two things before the month of February. I am (strangely enough) highly satisfied with both these things. The story *When the Sleeper Wakes* about the man who wakes up 200 years from now has assumed really noble proportions. It is twice as long as anything I have done before already, and I have done crowds of people, a revolutionary tumult, and a description of vast buildings and contrivances, in a way that even on a temperate rereading does not shame me.[1] Parts I have reshaped, rewritten and retyped time after time. *Love and Mr Lewisham*[2] too grows very slowly. I cut out four chapters as irrelevant in my last encounter. And there are symptoms of a play coming on,[3] but that shall not bar the way to Italy I swear. These things are the essentials of life. For the setting a mild muggy winter, and volumes in flow up to Dec 20th, and just a snap of frost and holiday at Christmas, with I re-

gret to say drunkenness on punch at the Swan at Leatherhead. We had our friends the Bowketts[4] with us at Christmas and for the rest of this twaddle, Mrs Wells has had a bureau of imposing proportions given her in recognition of her literary attainments. The chimneys

[1] After serialisation in the *Graphic*, *When the Sleeper Wakes* was published in May 1899. Wells later decided that it was poorly written because he was "overworked, and badly in need of a holiday." He revised it in 1910.

[2] *Love and Mr. Lewisham* was published in June 1900 after serialisation in the *Weekly Times*.

[3] With an eye to money Wells was for years interested in writing for the stage. In 1902 he tentatively planned to collaborate in a play with Arnold Bennett, and in 1904 he vainly submitted *Hoopdriver's Holiday*, a stage version of *The Wheels of Chance*, to Frederick Harrison, co-manager of the Haymarket Theatre.

[4] Sidney Bowkett (*c.* 1866–1936), a schoolmate of Wells, wrote several highly popular plays, among them *Lucky Miss Dean*. After 1916 Wells lost touch with Bowkett, who died in miserable poverty in Southwark.

still for the most part smoke, and we had a cheerful Christmas almanac of skeletons from the man Hick.

And now for the man Gissing. How goes his health? And after that how goes his work? Does that novel gather itself together?—the romance rather of Cassiodorus? When we do come to Italy we shall come in an earnest mood. What are the residential qualities of the country between Naples and Rome? What of Frascati? What could one do at Siena? I am sick of this damned climate and of my perpetual catarrh. What do you mean to do? Do you think of coming back, or settling on some Mons of Rome? If so we will be with you in five years time. I mean to lead a great multitude of selected people out of this reek, sooner or later, artists and writers and decent souls and we will all settle in little houses along and up a slope of sunlight all set with olives and vines and honey mellowed marble ruins between the mountains and the sea. There we will sit in the evening of our days dressed in decent blouses talking talking of this and that. Keep it in mind.

Yours ever

H. G. Wells.

Need I say—our warmest regards?

26

GISSING TO WELLS

6 *January* 1898 *Via del Boschetto*, 41 *A*, *Rome*

MY DEAR WELLS, Do you remember that long walk and talk we had one day, at Budleigh, when I told you something of my home troubles? I heartily wish I could have you here now, and talk to you about the same dreary subject—little as you may relish the thought. Things are going on very badly.[1] My wife has carried uproar into the house of the friend who was kind enough to take her; insult and fury are her return for infinite kindness and good-will; it seems impossible for her to remain there much longer. It wouldn't matter in the least, but for the poor little child who is with her; she might go where she liked, and rage to her heart's content. As it is, I fear I may be obliged to return to England much sooner than I meant to. I cannot shift my responsibilities onto the shoulders of people whose only fault is their desire to help me.

Of course I shall try to stay here until at least the end of March; for a change of climate before then would be a

[1] It was presumably at the suggestion of Miss Collett that Miss Eliza Orme had undertaken to care for Mrs Gissing and the son Alfred for £50 a quarter. Mrs Gissing's conduct was so violent that by February Miss Orme was compelled to lodge her charges elsewhere, and she advised Gissing to secure a legal separation.

risky matter. What I am to do when I come back is very doubtful. Miss Orme knows of a decent working-class woman, who could let part of her house unfurnished, and I think I shall have to compel the wretched creature to live there. With people of the educated class she cannot live—their proximity simply maddens her, in spite of every effort to win her good-will. I foresee that it will be necessary to take the child away; he might just as well be in the care of a drunkard or a lunatic, as of this furious and hateful woman.

I don't want you to write until that free day of which you speak. You cannot advise, cannot help. I tell you all about it, simply that you may not be surprised if I return suddenly to England.

It is bitterly cold here, and, just now, I am rather miserable—suffering from a sore-throat, from poverty, from all sorts of petty troubles. I see there is going to be a long, hard fight through the years that remain to me. I shall take lodgings for myself somewhere near London, and live there till I am driven away—which will be soon enough, no doubt. How would you relish literary labour under such conditions?

Remember me to your wife and to Mrs Robbins, and believe me, my dear boy,

Ever sincerely yours,

George Gissing

8 *January*

P.S. The arrival of your letter has led me to open this, and add a few lines. My position contrasts rather lugubriously with the pictures you draw, of present and future. I pass the days thinking over my accursed troubles, and wondering what I shall do.

None the less, it delights me (believe this) to hear of your successful work. I am sure it is good—very good. Bythebye, do send me a copy of your *War of the Worlds*. I beg for it, *in forma pauperis*. You shall have my dirty *Human Odds and Ends*,[1] and the Dickens volume, when I return.

If you seriously think of coming to Italy, let me, before you start, give you an itinerary. On the first visit, you will hardly be able to settle down anywhere; it will be all movement and sight-seeing. I shall hear from you again.

Every other day I have had bad, bad news from London.[2] I try to work at my old-world subject,[3] but of

[1] *Human Odds and Ends*, published in November 1898 by Lawrence and Bullen, was a collection of twenty-nine stories which originally appeared in the *English Illustrated Magazine* and the *Sketch* during the years 1893–95. Gissing's description of the book may be due to the fact that Clement Shorter, in commissioning the stories, asked Gissing to draw his subjects from "more or less disreputable life." (*The Private Life of Henry Maitland*, p. 91.)

[2] In *Experiment in Autobiography* Wells describes how the arrival in Rome of a letter from England threw Gissing into anger and despair.

[3] *Veranilda*.

course do very little. Probably I shall spend next Christmas in the workhouse.[1]

Ever yours,
G. G.

27

GISSING TO WELLS [postcard]

13 *January* 1898 *Via del Boschetto*, 41 *A*, *Rome*

Many thanks for your letter. I have decided to stay on—unless any very serious news should come. Things are bad, and no prospect of improving. The book will take at *least* 18 months more; so that, of course, something else will have to come before it.

Do you seriously think of coming south so soon? It is very cold here, and cheerless. But I forget that you see things in a brighter light, and have so much more energy.[2]

[1] Morley Roberts says that Gissing's perpetual references to Marylebone Workhouse used to worry W. H. Hudson. (*W. H. Hudson: A Portrait* (1924), p. 52.) In this instance, however, Gissing was in earnest: his earnings for the year just ended were £101. 13s. 4d.

[2] *Veranilda* was incomplete at Gissing's death. It is not clear whether Gissing had "something else" definitely in mind. Writing to his sister on 7 December 1897 he expressed the need to get to work and spoke of having the "materials for a good little book." (*Letters of George Gissing to His Family*, p. 359.) This was probably *By the Ionian Sea*, which he did not actually begin until 28 June 1899. The financial pressure on Gissing was lightened by

You have quite enough to do. Don't trouble about this business. It will be the same to the end.

Excuse card. Haven't force of mind enough to write a letter.

Yours,
G. G.

28

WELLS TO GISSING

22 *January* 1898 *Heatherlea, Worcester Park*

MY DEAR GISSING, Thanks very much for your card. But as for weather—good Lord!—if you could only see the mist dripping from this damned brown grey avenue outside my windows. My one pleasure, our only pleasure is an old Murray we have got from the London Library wherein is a map of Roma.[1] I pore over the thumbed sheets marking the Corso, tracing my way over the bridge to the Piazza San Pietro and the Vatican, returning for a ride on that electric tramway (is it?) to the Villa

---

the advance he received on *The Town Traveller*. (See Letter 33.) In any case, it appears that Gissing did not begin his next published work, *The Crown of Life*, until July 1898.

[1] In the margin Wells wrote: "Where is your infernal street? It would be a great gratification to mark the place on the map with a blot or something. It is not my map, but the L.L's."

Borghese. In spirit we have already crossed the bridge of St Angelo together, and traced the Servian walls across the wastes of the Aventine. But buses by the Colosseum! and a chunk of the wall of Servius by the railway station? I like the little steps up and down by the Capitol, and all the wilderness of lumber[?] to the south east of it as well as any part of Roma so far. We will do some glorious loafing my man! The more I see of these Murrays the more I settle to Rome. Naples seems to me too much volcano and scene painting—a jaunt—a place where loafing is impossible because of lazzaroni, and as for Florence! I'd sooner Winchester any day. But I conceive of a day or so in the gardens of the Villa Borghese, spring sunlight, cigarettes, and an intermittent uneventful friendly conversation and down in that south west corner, between the river and the Colosseum and the walls, there must be places *made* for loafing. There you must tell me all the flesh you have put on the bare bones of that story[1] of the sunset and the coming of the wild men again. I'm not coming to Rome a sight seeing. I don't care a triturated damn for all the blessed oil paintings in the world, and precious little for the sculpture, and I'm not going to be made to go and see places I shouldn't go to see if I lived in Rome. The *Jesu* may go crucify itself and all such (if you will pardon me) bloody places. I'm coming to see Rome and yourself, and I don't mean to fall into the snare of the tourist and not see the city for its sights. But

[1] *Veranilda.*

speaking of the sights of Rome—have you seen something like this about. If so—shoot it! It's not human.

It's Hall Caine. 

His damned infernal —— (word erased [1]—Madam coming upstairs) book—*The Christian* (When Mrs H. G. Wells comes home—she is out—she will insist on seeing this letter and then the Lord have mercy upon me!). His damned infernal (as above) book has sold 100,000 (one hundred thousand) copies. One hundred thousand copies.[2]

100,000

Otherwise he has no claim upon our attention. But speaking of this topic I have been learning wonderful things of publishing these last few weeks or so. I have found out *how it is done*. But that secret is for your private ear. Suffice it that I do not think I shall allow you to go larking about with that romance of yours. So soon as it is anywhere near being done I am going to take it away from you and I myself personally (no agents) am going to

[1] The blotted word is *bloody*.

[2] The popular success of *The Christian* was due not only to Caine's tasteless mixing of melodrama and morality but to the advertising methods of the publisher.

serialise and arrange the terms of publication for you. It is a thing I can do extremely well. The refinement of my mind, and the tactical necessity of a Spenlow to my Jorkins [1] compel me to do my business through Pinker. But your book and your position are for a more delicate mind than his. Worked properly—my dear man—worked properly—that book if only it fulfils its promise will be worth £600 down and an almost inevitable *boom*. God blight my liver if I lie! Not that these things really matter! The point is—is it good and going shapely? I'm having awful times with my beggar.[2] He won't shape. The fact of it is its gotten just at the top of my powers or a little beyond em! So I'm midway between a noble performance and a noble disaster. I've just had the typewritten copy home again, and I have been tearing out chapters, inserting chapters, marking chapters to be reshaped and rewritten. But there are nice things—a *crèche*, a circumstantial description of flying, a beautiful phonographic newspaper with a leathery flat voice, the finest architecture conceivable, set with advertisements from top to base, a pleasure city, logical development of Margit the germ,[3] and all sorts of pretty fittings.

[1] Partners in *David Copperfield.* Jorkins seldom appeared, and all disagreeable decisions were attributed to him by Spenlow.

[2] *When the Sleeper Wakes.*

[3] There is nothing in the book to answer to this phrase; Wells admitted that he "scamped the finish" of *When the Sleeper Wakes.* (*Experiment in Autobiography*, VIII, 4.)

And returning to that holiday. So far as I can see we shall set out about the last week in February. We shall come straight to Rome, I think. There we want quarters for a month, near you if you'll stand the annoyance. I expect we'd better do an hotel, but I hate hotels where they do things in the magnificent vein. Any advice will be received with gratitude. Also we are at Lesson 4 in Sauer's *Italian Conversation Grammar*.

The Lord bless and keep you.

Yours ever

H. G. WELLS

1 Ho la penna della zia.

2 I zii hanno i cavalli degli angeli.

?

3 La fanciulla avena quadro maritozzi.

4 La fanciulla ela sorella del padre.[1]

[1] I have the pen of my aunt.
The uncles have the horses of the angels.
The young girl had four buns.
The young girl is the sister of the father.

29

GISSING TO WELLS

27 *January* 1898 *Via del Boschetto*, 41 *A*, *Rome*

MY DEAR WELLS, If this letter looks wobbly, the reason is that I am just getting over an attack of influenza. I have been in an infernal state.[1]

With extraordinary brutality, I never acknowledged the receipt of your portrait. Many thanks for it, now that I am reminded of the matter by the arrival of that of Mrs Wells. Yours I like pretty well—it is yourself, but might, I think, be more agreeably characteristic. Your wife's is delightful. The good smiling little face! May it smile, and look just as youthful, for many a long year to come!

Of course your last letter rejoices me. Let me tell you how the practical arrangements seem to me best settled. It will have to be a hotel. A boarding-house is always unpleasant, and private lodgings are forbidden by the language difficulty. The best hotel will be the *Minerva*, close by the Pantheon—a really comfortable place; I have stayed there. Unfortunately there is no medium in Rome between grandeur and squalor, but the Minerva is the

[1] Writing to his sister Ellen on January 23 Gissing declared, "My experience is that people with a weak chest should *not* come to Italy. For invalids it offers little comfort and many dangers." (*Letters of George Gissing to His Family*, p. 364.)

quietest of the first-rate houses. All languages are spoken there.

As to terms. You two, having a comfortable room, and eating at table-d'hote, ought to manage it, I think, for about 10 francs a day each; but I will make express inquiries. At less than this, I fear it cannot anywhere be done with a lady—that is, in the cosmopolitan hotels, to which we are restricted in this case. It will probably be best for you to arrange to omit the luncheon, and eat wherever you may happen to be in Rome. In that case, perhaps it will be less than 10 francs. I will let you know.

And now for another matter. I find myself beaten. I have to do, as a middle-aged invalid, what I did easily enough when young and healthy; and it has been a hideous mistake. I have gravely injured my health; I have lost my time;—and I have saved £20! It must come to an end, this kind of life I am leading. So, what say you if I, too, take a room at the Minerva? I shall probably do so in a fortnight's time.

In fact, if I did not, we should see very little of each other. I dare not go out after dark, and you could not come hither, leaving your wife alone. You could not bring her, as I have only my bedroom (which, you know, it is the Italian custom to use for all purposes). Long walks I cannot take, for I am getting miserably weak. Now it would be an absurd thing for you and me to be in Rome together, and never enjoy an evening's talk! To save my life, and to secure this end, I shall go to the Minerva, where I shall find the comforts of civilization. Don't think you will necessarily see me morning, noon and night. You will be perfectly independent. Of course I shall be working a good deal.—But you and I, my dear boy, will never be in Rome again together, and we must make the most of the time.

There is a very good "common room." Private sitting-rooms are very expensive.[1]

Let me have your views of all this.

As to money, you must reckon that 26 francs [lire] (and a little more) go to the English pound. So that 10 lire are only about 8/6—isn't it so?

To give you some idea of what I have endured here, I had a roast fowl the other day (after my fever), and the landlady (good, beastly creature) *tore it up* before me with her fingers—never touching knife or fork. It almost made me sick, in my queasy state.[2] But that is a trifle—many worse things have to be borne here, and yet the house is well furnished and considered very respectable. —No, no; I must go back to the Europeans. These lower-class Italians are Oriental in their savagery.

This street is on right-hand side of Via Nazionale, just beyond the Bank of Italy, going n.e. *just* beyond the Via del Serpenti.[3]

[1] These two sentences are written in the margin of the preceding paragraph.

[2] An exactly similar experience in the inn at Cotrone also offended Gissing's sensibility. (*By the Ionian Sea*, Chapter X.)

[3] This sentence is written in the margin.

Now about your route. Do you want to stop at Paris? If not, you miss it altogether, taking a ticket from Charing Cross to Rome *via*: Dover, Calais, Laon, Belfort, the St Gotthard, Milan and Florence. I implore you to come by this route. There are two most glorious bits of it the passage of the St Gotthard, and the passage of the Apennines from Bologna to Florence. Of course you will break the journey, and *you must do so in such a way as to have those two bits during day time*. All this will be arranged for you at Gage's office, where you can best get the through ticket. Don't attempt to get it at Charing Cross.[1]

As you probably know, the quick trains never have a third class. But I suppose you would not use it, even if they had. The seconds are admirable, and used by all but the wealthiest people.

Get the S.E.R. Continental Time-Book. It has full tables and information.

(Dover to Calais, 50 minutes—hardly time to be sick.)

A good place for passing the night is Milan. But I think you ought to take two rests. Any number are allowed.

You can only book your luggage as far as to the Italian frontier (Chiasso). After that, *all luggage*, except what you take into the carriage, has to be paid for. Book the trunk at Charing X to Chiasso, where it will have to be

[1] The actual itinerary of the Wellses is thus described in Catherine Wells's diary: Monday March 7; 7:41 start from Worcester Park; 4:50 Paris; 8 Dijon; Tuesday March 8; 5 Modane; 7 a.m. The Alps; 12 Genoa; 4 Pisa; 10:50 Rome.

examined by the Custom House and rebooked to Rome. You will not see it till that point of the journey.[1]

Of course I shall write again about many things.

Remember me very kindly to Mrs Wells and to Mrs Robbins—who perhaps will recall my name.

Ever yours,

GEORGE GISSING

30

WELLS TO GISSING

[31 *January* 1898] *Heatherlea, Worcester Park*

HONOURED SIR, We rejoice at the idea of the Minerva with you. I have looked it up in Murray and it seems just the place for us. Murray says we must get a room at the top to be sunny. It would be unwise to arrange for full board but the bedroom, attendance, breakfast and dinner we might properly arrange by the week—for four weeks, —say 100 to 120 lire the two of us. But there's no need to haggle. Lunch shall be a series in experiments in gastronomy—the Lord help us! About coming—we had thought of the train-de-luxe Calais–Rome express. It takes 37 hours from Charing X to Rome—saving a day out of our lives and all the furies and exasperations of stoppages. Customs on board. Refreshment carriage on

[1] This letter, with its detailed information and counsel, hardly squares with the opinion of Wells and Roberts that Gissing was inept in all practical matters.

train. It comes by Mt Cenis. As we are very anxious to get to you as soon as possible we want to come by that, but if you forbid Well!—

We shall stop a clear month in Rome. Dull, cold and wet days will do for churches galleries and such. But the spring sunshine will be about and on such days the open air. One bright day we will train to Marino and walk over Cavo to Albano a whole day—and another shall see us at Riofreddo and over the hill to Cerreto Romano with a bottle of wine and hard boiled eggs or such in a basket. And one day we will go along the Appian way with a similar basket and an attentive driver to Frattochie. And once Veii. We will have some purple times. And when the month is over we shall go on to Naples—or stop longer, as we may decide at the time. We shall stop about Naples for three weeks, stopping two or three days at a time at Cava, Amalfi, Sorrento, Capri, and Castelmarre and finally return by the Orient steamboat from Naples. We've cut out Florence from the scheme. It will do somewhen else. As for you, you must get yourself into training to come. I hope I shan't be too much of the idle apprentice, compared with you. I have two or three short stories to write—Rome should be inspiring.[1]

Yours ever

H. G. WELLS

[1] "Walking through some fields near Tivoli the *Story of Miss Winchelsea's Heart* came into my head." (*Experiment in Autobiography*, VIII, 3.)

31

GISSING TO WELLS

5 *February* 1898 *Via del Boschetto*, 41 *A*

MY DEAR WELLS, I have had a terrific morning!—The Minerva *will not do*. They want 12 lire a day, for one person, without wine; they refuse to let me engage a room even for a single day in advance; they are swarming with people; and, finally, the whole building is heated to 70° F., a most dangerous state of things.

Heaven be thanked, I have done better. Near the Piazza di Spagna (best part of town) is the Hotel Alibert, kept by a German. I went through the place, saw rooms, sanitary quarters, etc., and all was good. Well, they will let you two have a nice double-bedded room, with sun, and complete board (a bottle of wine for each person daily) for 17 lire a day. Whenever you like to miss the lunch, they will charge only 14 lire. This, understand, for *both* of you. It is really very cheap. Excellent dining room, meals good, and large drawing and smoking rooms. Simply because the place does not have a fashionable name. At the first-class hotels, they ask 16 lire a day for each person, without wine. Rome is simply *packed* with foreigners, and they tell me that in another month people will find it very difficult to get lodgings of any kind.

Well, *I* shall go to the Alibert on the 14 of Feb., and

test it for you. They will charge 9 lire a day, including 1 bottle of wine. (Bythebye, the place has a good bathing-establishment attached to it.)

I entreat you to write *instantly*, and to say whether you will take my word for this hotel. It is really clean and comfortable, and very convenient in situation. Omitting lunch, it will cost you 98 l. a week, all told. I can engage your room for you, if you approve. I feel convinced you will prefer it to the Minerva.

Ever yours,
GEORGE GISSING

Delighted with *The War of the Worlds*.[1] Devoured it at a sitting. You are a fine fellow!

32

WELLS TO GISSING

[*c.* 9 *February* 1898][2]

DEAR GISSING, Certainly! The Hotel Alibert—well spoken of by Murray. We shall come March 7th (Monday) from London reaching Rome 10:30 on Tuesday night, and take a fly straight to the hotel. As the train is sometimes three or four hours late—don't wait up for us.

[1] Published in January 1898.

[2] In the upper margin Wells wrote: "What is the language spoken in that hotel by the servants? We would like to learn enough to ask for things."

We shall go straight to bed and meet you at *déjeuner* Wednesday. So fix things up for that date. I expect we'll leave for Easter but if not of course there is no objection on our part to a rise of prices. What a bother we are being to you!

Yours ever
H. G.

33

GISSING TO WELLS

18 *February* 1898 *Hotel Alibert*, *Rome*

MY DEAR WELLS, I am glad to be able to assure you that this hotel does very well indeed. The food is remarkably good: excellently cooked, and all dishes of such stuff as a man may get nutriment from. One thing only may trouble you. It is the custom in Italy to take only coffee and bread and butter at breakfast; here, honey is added; but I am afraid you may want more, to start upon your day's wandering. I am sure you could easily arrange to have eggs.

The servants seem to speak *all* languages. As a matter of principle, I speak Italian, and, if you have time, I strongly advise you to get up a few Italian words and phrases—seeing that you can hardly do without them in going about town and country.

I wish your train arrived at a more reasonable hour.

But of course everything shall be neatly arranged for you, and I shall look forward to the next morning with extreme delight.

I feel decidedly better since I have been here. Of course I have fever, and a bad cold, and a furious cough, and can do absolutely nothing; but this is the chronic state of things.

I have seen reviews of your book in *Spectator* and *Saturday*—given me by friends here. I have also, unfortunately, seen the *Athenaeum*.[1] Now, can you tell me (in moments of extreme idleness one wishes to know such things) who the people are who review fiction for the *Athenaeum*? Are they women, soured by celibacy and by ineffectual attempts to succeed as authors? Even as they treat you this time, they have consistently treated me,[2]

[1] The *Saturday Review* of 29 January 1898 and the *Spectator* of the same date praised *The War of the Worlds* in the highest terms—"thrilling effect," "remarkable refinement," and "most original." The reviewer in the *Spectator* singled out for special approval the "moral effects" which Wells achieved in the description of the stampede of Londoners along the Great North Road when the Martians invaded the city. The review in the *Athenaeum* (5 February 1898) dismissed *The War of the Worlds* as "vulgar and commonplace" and declared that instead of rising to the opportunity of describing the exodus from London Wells was content with "the cheap emotions of a few bank clerks and newspaper touts, and the jostling in the road which might very well do for an account of a Derby crowd going to Epsom."

[2] A sampling of ten *Athenaeum* reviews from 1887 to 1896 suggests that Gissing was unduly sensitive and resentful. To be sure there were frequent references to the "exceedingly painful" subject-matter and the "depressing tone" of his novels, but there was

—one continuous snarl and sneer. They are beastly creatures—I can think of no other term.

Will you believe me when I tell you that Colles has got an *advance* of £250 from Methuen's for a novel of mine, and £100 advance from America?[1] I am quite serious. I wrote the thing for serialization, but Colles could not place it before 1902, and I could not wait. Heaven be thanked, I am now certain of being able to spend the month with you in Rome. I had secretly feared that I should have to bid you goodbye before you left, through lack of cash. Silence!

I shall have much to tell you, my dear old boy. But

---

also praise of Gissing's "sane and delicate" treatment of such characters as Godwin Peak, and the occasional "genuinely tragic effects." Furthermore, Gissing might have profited from a point repeatedly made in the *Athenaeum*—and one also made by Henry James and Arnold Bennett—namely, that his novels lacked focus as a result of the needless dialogue, superfluous characters, and too numerous episodes. According to Morley Roberts, Gissing was stung by what he described as "a careful and well-written attack" on him in the *Spectator*. (*The Private Life of Henry Maitland*, p. 236.) This was a review (14 September 1895) of *Eve's Ransom* which declared that the novel, though interesting and well-written, was marred by Gissing's refusal to "select the highest type of humanity for his subject."

[1] William Morris Colles (1855–1926), a barrister who specialised in the legal intricacies of copyright, founded the Author's Syndicate in 1890. Among his clients were Meredith, Hardy, Barrie, and Hall Caine. The novel Gissing referred to was *The Town Traveller*, and the American publisher was F. A. Stokes. The advances on this book represented an appreciable improvement over Gissing's earnings from previous novels—for example, £50 from *A Life's Morning* (1888) and £150 from *New Grub Street* (1891).

have no fear; it can be exhausted in one talk; and after that your holiday shall not be interfered with.

Let me advise you to bring both warm and light clothing. You are coming to the most treacherous climate in Europe. Everyone here, with thermometer sometimes at 75°, dresses as though for an arctic winter, and it is absolutely necessary. Of course every day the weather improves, but sudden changes are always to be looked for. Do be very careful on the journey. If you get here with a cold, you will never shake it off. The Express will of course be over-warmed. Take care when you get out for a few moments at a station.

It is almost too good to be true—the thought of our having a second spring holiday all together. Well, well; fate is artful in with-holding us from despair. Let us do our best not to quarrel. It would be a hateful thing to have disagreeable memories of Rome, due to such a cause.

Kindest remembrances to Mrs Wells, and to Mrs Robbins.

Yours ever,
GEORGE GISSING

34

WELLS TO GISSING

[*c.* 23 *February* 1898]

MY DEAR GISSING, Your letter when we return from a muddy little walk in which we have been indulging in anticipation of a walk up the steps and the view of Rome from the Medici Gardens, then down to the Piazza del Populo—Corso and so forth. Temper on the part of Mrs Wells (as usual). This time because I insisted on at least glimpsing the Colosseum the first day—while she (very foolishly) wanted to see the Castle of S Angelo where her favourite historical character Benvenuto Cellini fired the gun. If she cannot see that Inn with the sign of the Sun there will be a fearful row. Is it still there? If not for God's sake do something in the matter. But my dear chap, I'm glad indeed to know there's to be no separation before the holiday is over. The prices Colles has got you are none so ill but nothing wonderful for you especially as the rates are rising all round just now and especially for contemporary fiction. It isn't half what you deserve. But he's an ass not to serialise it. Such a paper as *Today* could plank down a hundred anyhow. However—! When is the book coming? If you get £450[1] for this brief effort, what will you get for that

[1] In the preceding letter Gissing stated that the sum was £350.

Cassiodorus romance? You're only dawning. The *Athenaeum* doesn't matter a damn. I know it's spiteful and unjust, it irritates reviewers elsewhere into unseemly praise, and it makes no impression on sales. But that's no sour woman's work—that's a man. (Please God) I know it is a man. I have always as a matter of conscience insulted schoolmasters, London professorlings, Sir Walter Bezant (or Besant), Rider Haggard, Crockett, Professor Judd, and the pseudo artist as distinguished from the man Caine.[1] After a time that sort of thing comes back a little. But not injuriously. And for the most part I have had reviews which only my regard for your regard of our native language prevents my calling phenomenal.

I'm glad indeed to hear of the goodness of the Alibert. Everything points to a gorgeous time now imminent. I've got to finish a story before I come but it's going at a great pace now and little more to do.

Mrs Wells in a great rage again—tea has been ready some time. After tea the rule is work.

Yours ever

H. G.

[1] Sir Walter Besant (1836–1901) was the author of numerous historical romances; Sir Henry Rider Haggard (1856–1925) achieved wide success with his African romances; Samuel Rutherford Crockett (1860–1914) exploited Scottish regionalism in *The Stickit Minister* and other novels. John Judd (1840–1916), for many years Professor of Geology in the Royal College of Science, is the subject of a chapter in *Experiment in Autobiography*.

35

GISSING TO WELLS [postcard]

1 *March* 1898 *Rome*

All is arranged. The hotel Omnibus will be at the station to meet your train; just ask for "Omnibus dell' Hotel Alibert," as you leave the station. If train should be *very* late,[1] and omnibus gone, of course take carriage. The distance is considerable.

Many thanks for your kind note about *C.D.*[2]

I look forward eagerly to seeing you both.

G. G.

36

MRS WELLS TO GISSING

18 *May* [1898] *Heatherlea, Worcester Park, Surrey*

DEAR MR GISSING, It seems very dreadful to reflect that we have sent you absolutely nothing but one meagre postcard since we left Rome. This came to me with particular point just now because I was getting into a fine

[1] The Wellses arrived on March 8 at 10:50 p.m., only twenty minutes late.

[2] *Charles Dickens: A Critical Study* was published in February 1898 by Blackie.

mess with your portrait (by Rothenstein)[1] and some gum and a piece of cardboard. So I will at least let you have the facts about us. After leaving you we spent but three days in Naples, and escaped hastily out of the dirt and noise of it to Capri for a week. Then Naples again for a week and Pompeii for the same time. Vesuvius was duly ascended and from Pompeii we had a glorious excursion to Amalfi via a lot of other places, and another to Paestum,[2] which I think we remember with the greatest delight of all. While at Naples one of our most delightful days was spent on Mrs Foley's[3] island—they entertained us charmingly. Then after we had been at Pompeii a week we had the very disappointing news that there was no room for us on the *Orient* steamer. We were so much unhinged by this that we packed hastily and in less than an hour left for Naples, whence we started northwards again at 6 the next morning.

As a scrap of consolation we went to Florence that day and spent three days there. So it came about that at midday we were passing through Rome again, and H. G. says it was all a pretty trick played us by the Trevi foun-

[1] In his diary for 7 June 1897 Gissing wrote: "Went to keep appointment with W. Rothenstein, at his studio, Glebe Place, Chelsea. He made two drawings of me; one sitting, the other standing—latter I liked best." It is reproduced opposite.

[2] Paestum appears in the later pages of Wells's "A Dream of Armageddon" (1901).

[3] Mrs Nelson Foley was a sister of Conan Doyle. In the diary of the Italian journey Mrs Wells made the following entry for April 24: "Lunch and tea at Isola de Gailo with Foley's."

GEORGE GISSING

The second drawing by Sir William Rothenstein

tain. You remember our spells with the Soldi. That night we went out to find the Duomo. We came suddenly upon the Campanile round a corner. I nearly cried, it was so beautiful, and in the moonlight, so terrifying. Our emotions would have pleased you had you seen us then. I fancy we seemed a bit stoney sometimes in Rome. In the three days we did not see much of course but we saw all the pictures we knew best, and went into Dante's house and up the Campanile. The third day of our stay the rioting was growing serious. We stumbled upon Mr Turner in the street that day and by arrangement met him by the Duomo in the evening to go to a café.[1] But all cafés were closed and every window closely shuttered. Bands of carabinieri were parading the streets encouraged by a nervous little officer with a drawn sword! and the streets were all crowded with silent people. We saw what we could of it—there was some stone throwing but the smallest offender was instantly chased and seized and marched off with four revolvers at his head.

Later there was some shooting—the police seem to have lost their heads. The next day, Sunday, May 8th we started from Florence at 6 in the morning for Milan meaning to stay the night there. Happily at Bologna we bought a paper and learnt about the rioting there, so very fortunately we determined to push on for Chiasso and

[1] Reginald Turner (1869–1938), who had a wide acquaintance in literary circles, was a close friend of Oscar Wilde and Max Beerbohm.

Lugano. If we had not done this, unless we had been stopped at the station, we should probably have been shut up in Milan two or three days. They say our train was the last to leave. To Lucerne the next day, Brussels the next and home the next finished our journey, to our great joy—we were very homesick.

I hope this will reach you soon and that you will write and tell us what you have been doing since we left you. I have a cheerful postcard from the young ladies of *Porth*[1] or should I spell it *Porreth*? announcing their immediate arrival in London. There seems to be no other news to tell you of. We are both extremely brown and well of course. Warmest greetings from H. G.

Yours sincerely

CATHERINE WELLS

37

MRS WELLS TO GISSING

[*c.* 24 *May* 1898] *Heatherlea, Worcester Park*

DEAR MR GISSING, We have run Mr Evans[2] to earth in London and he is coming down to spend the evening on

[1] The Scotchwomen are presumably the ones alluded to in a letter of 22 August 1898 from W. M. Evans to Mrs Wells. Speaking of "Roman friends" he reported that he had visited "the Steels" in Edinburgh. Mrs Wells's engagement book lists "Miss F. and A. Steel, 59 Castle Street, Edinburgh."

[2] In the upper margin H. G. Wells wrote: "Dear Gissing, Evans!—but madam will tell you." Mrs Wells then added: "Evans *is coming*." For Evans see Letter 55, note 2.

Gissing, Hornung, Conan Doyle and Wells in Rome

Saturday next. Now we *should* be delighted if you would come too. Please think if you can come, for it would be delightful to gather once more and would be quite "one more day snatched from Fate" as you used to say. And you needn't toil back to Dorking at night. We can put you up of course. Now if you will come we shall shout for joy.

It is most excellent that you have settled so near us,[1] and we shall certainly come and see you when you are ready for us. But meanwhile let us have a gossip on Saturday.

Last Saturday the ladies from Perth spent the evening with us, and we had much hilarity. Dr Doyle[2] is staying in the same hotel as Mr Evans—Morley's—and we have asked him to come down—but cannot promise him for Saturday. Still the menu should tempt you without him.

If you will say you are coming I will look out your trains—that ought to settle it!

Yours very sincerely,

CATHERINE WELLS

[1] Gissing had taken a house in Dorking. In selecting it he hoped to keep his whereabouts a secret from his wife; but see Letter 79.

[2] Conan Doyle concluded an undated letter to Wells: "Saw Gissing last week at Hornung's." See illustration opposite.

38

GISSING TO MRS WELLS

26 *May* 1898 7 *Clifton Terrace*, *Dorking*

DEAR MRS WELLS, I am of all men most miserable. You *know* how gladly I would come, but I have an engagement which holds me from Friday to Tuesday. The thing is impossible.

I laughed with delight in your letter. How fine it is, this meeting of people who unaffectedly are glad to meet! I would walk twenty miles to talk with the brave Evans, or with those splendid Scotch women. But some day I shall see them all. What an evening you must have had, last Saturday! I can hear them and see them, the good, honest, refreshing creatures.

Do remember me very warmly to Evans, and all good be with him.

You have seen Paestum.[1] Nay, but we will shout together over that before long.

I have a 10-page type-written letter from a stranger, in which, oddly enough, occurs mention of H. G. You shall see the thing.

Always, sincerely yours,

GEORGE GISSING

[1] Paestum figures in *The Emancipated*, especially Part II, Chapter 6; and it is the subject of a stylised passage in *The Private Papers of Henry Ryecroft*, "Autumn," XIX–XX.

39

GISSING TO WELLS

22 June 1898 *7 Clifton Terrace, Dorking*

MY DEAR WELLS, I really must see you. Will you—you and your wife—face the awkward journey, and come over some afternoon to stay a 7 o'clock meal? I know it is asking a great deal, but I am in the usual gloom (nay, worse than usual[1]) and I really must talk to you. Appoint your own day.[2]

I heard that Mrs Williams was coming to see you last Saturday.[3] Did you have a good evening?

Yours always,

GEORGE GISSING

Of course I want you to see my house.

[1] In the hope of making money Gissing in early June attempted to write a play. After two false beginnings he started afresh on June 15, but after a week of "desperate struggle" he abandoned the effort. (Gordan, *George Gissing*, p. 36.)

[2] The back of the letter bears the following pencilled note in the hand of Mrs Wells: "H.G. will cycle to reach you about 3 by Leatherhead Road. Return before 7."

[3] Mrs Rosalind Williams, the youngest sister of Beatrice Webb, met Gissing and the Wellses in Rome and kept in touch with the latter for two years. Writing to Mrs Wells on 23 December 1899, Mrs Williams recalled, "I often think of the pleasant times we all had together in Rome. I have not heard anything of Mr Gissing for such a long time. I often wonder what has happened to him for I got his new book *The Crown of Life* from the library and thought it exceedingly good."

40

GISSING TO WELLS

26 *June* 1898 7 *Clifton Terrace, Dorking*

MY DEAR H. G., An unforeseen difficulty has arisen. My housekeeper objects to being left alone in the house for even a single night, and it isn't yet clear how this obstacle is to be got over. However, she has a female relative at Reigate, who may possibly be induced to come and stay with her.

Medical examination still goes on. Latest report: decided phthisis (though not very active)—strong gouty tendency—uncertainty of heart—bad emphysema—liver at any moment to give serious trouble—disposition to eczema. It's all rather discouraging.

However, cycling in moderation is strongly recommended, and I shall [*illegible*] my endeavour to come to you next Saturday. To-morrow (Monday) I go to London.

I have just had a letter from Mrs Lambert,[1] dated Hampton Court Palace. She and husband are going to live at a farm, at Milford near Godalming. Much bitterness expressed because I have neglected to write.

I have a fine, lurid idea. Could it be given out that I

[1] Mrs Wells's diary for the Italian holiday has the following entry for March 11 and April 4: "To tea with Mrs Lambert."

am *dead*? Then, with comfort of half a dozen intimates, I might work steadily for a year or two, preparing posthumous books.

Yours ever,
G. G.

41

GISSING TO WELLS

29 *June* 1898 7 *Clifton Terrace, Dorking*

MY DEAR H. G., After all, the easiest arrangement, I find, will be for me to come to you on *Thursday* of next week and stay, if you will let me, till Sunday night or possibly Monday morning. I am vexed by this unforeseen hampering of my movements, but of course I have to admit that my housekeeper would not find it very pleasant to remain here absolutely alone for several days and nights. Stay she must, on account of my letters, and her relative can come Thursday—not before.

If this does not interfere with any plan of yours, merely keep silence.

Yours ever,
G. G.

42

GISSING TO WELLS

30 *June* 1898 7 *Clifton Terrace, Dorking*

MY DEAR H. G., Of course you are right, and I am unpardonable. It is monstrous to have given you this trouble after your extraordinary kindness in the matter. I will come on Saturday afternoon.

For the machine which you have hired purposely I insist (if necessary with oaths) on paying.[1]

Yours, with shame,

G. G.

[1] With respect to Gissing's cycling Wells recalled, "I tried to make him a cyclist, for he took no exercise at all except walking, and I thought it might be pleasant to explore Surrey and Sussex with him, but he was far too nervous and excitable to ride. It was curious to see this well-built Viking, blowing and funking as he hopped behind his machine. 'Get on to your ironmongery,' said I. He mounted, wobbled a few yards, and fell off shrieking with laughter. 'Ironmongery!' he gasped. 'Oh! riding on ironmongery!' and lay in the grass at the roadside, helpless with mirth." (*Experiment in Autobiography*, VIII, 3.)

43

GISSING TO WELLS

16 *July* 1898 *Dorking*

DEAR OLD BOY, Hearty thanks for good words and for criticism.—In "Justice and Vagabond" you will notice that the man's death is prepared for in the first sentence: the thing is a bit of irony—things postponed till too late —energy at the useless moment.[1]—As for "Out of the Fashion", why, you and I differ to a certain extent on the one great subject.[2] Of course I have bungled what I meant; but the sentiment is ingrained in me, and will outstand every assault of humour.—Never mind. Better than literature is honest friendliness.

[1] In "The Justice and the Vagabond," one of the better stories in *Human Odds and Ends*, an itinerant painter is brought before a magistrate, who recognises him as a schoolmate of thirty years since. Though living in easy circumstances the magistrate has been frustrated in every way by his wife who, at the moment, is absent from home. His desire to travel is revived by the talk of the vagabond, and the two men plan a trip to South America. But the magistrate dies in his sleep on the eve of their intended departure. The first sentence of the story reads, "Mr Rutland did not feel well this morning."

[2] "Out of the Fashion," the last story in *Human Odds and Ends*, is a thin chronicle of a wife who cheerfully sacrifices for her husband and children. It concludes, "An old-fashioned figure, out of harmony with the day that rules, and to our so modern eyes perhaps the oddest of the whole series of human odds and ends."

With no little chuckling I have read "Snooks."[1] There is much of your right self in this, and I enjoy the end.—I shall read *Mr Lewisham* with immense curiosity.

Terribly hot for cycling. I can now ride perfectly with one hand, waving the other wildly, or even extracting things from pocket. Fly in the eye has happened, and been overcome without pause.

But I have hideous nights of sleeplessness, and wonder how the *devil* I am to live this life much longer.[2]

Ever yours,

G. G.

Bythebye, you spell *Baedeker*[3] with two *k*'s, and I have taken the liberty to extract one of them throughout.

[1] In "Miss Winchelsea's Heart," a story about a party of British tourists in Italy, Mr Snooks's declaration of love is rejected by Miss Winchelsea because she cannot stand his name. When Fanny, another member of the party, makes known her dislike of the name, Mr Snooks promptly changes it to Se'noks (Sevenoaks), and they marry. Gissing's enjoyment of the story was no doubt connected with the fact which Wells recalled in a later prefatory note: " 'Miss Winchelsea's Heart' came into my head to tell my friend George Gissing on the Pincio one spring morning in 1898." (The Atlantic Edition, VI.)

[2] The sleeplessness was caused by eczema which was aggravated by Gissing's futile first attempts to write *The Crown of Life*. (Gordan, *George Gissing*, p. 36.)

[3] Miss Winchelsea, anxious to avoid looking "touristy," conceals her glaring red Baedeker in a grey cover.

44

GISSING TO WELLS

19 *July* 1898 7 *Clifton Terrace, Dorking*

MY DEAR H. G., I have suddenly fallen upon a mood of work—such as comes very rarely in these latter days. I labour all day long, and thank Heaven for the chance of doing so—dreading the slightest interruption.

But, as I know it will not last without some sort of change to help me, I shall come over to you on Saturday. *Not* cycling, for I shall return by the 10.25 that night. No comment or objection, I *entreat*. My ways are peculiar, and it is fatal to me not to have my own course just when I am fretting through a bit of imagination.[1]

Don't reply. Just keep very quiet, and let me walk into the house and out of it again, as little observed as possible.

Yours always,
G. G.

[1] On July 10 Gissing began to plan *The Crown of Life*. As was so often the case, the initial stages of composition were marked by frustration, scrapping of manuscripts, and repeated fresh beginnings. He was so discouraged that he laid aside *The Crown of Life* for some months.

45

GISSING TO WELLS [postcard]

27 *July* 1898 *Dorking*

No wonder. I too sink under the stifling air. Many thanks for O'D's[1] letters etc.—Delightful day with Mlle Fleury yesterday.[2]—I will write at length very soon. G. G.

(Please let H. G. send card to Hersey, asking him to send *me* a card when bicycle is ready. I will give Hersey cheque at once.)

[1] Brian Ború Dunne, a young American, met Gissing in Siena, where they lived in the same *pension*, and later met him daily in Rome at Fiorelli's restaurant. The relation between them may be glimpsed in the opening sentences of two letters which Dunne wrote to Wells many years later: "Do you remember George Gissing's friend who made you walk up five flights of stairs in Via Gregoriano in Rome in 1898: who played (?) the zither for your benefit, with Gissing remarking, 'You're out of practice my boy!' " "Do you remember your old traveling companion of Rome—pupil of George Gissing?" In 1914 Dunne published a book, *Cured! the 70 Adventures of a Dyspeptic*, with a foreword by Wells. At the present time (1959) Dunne, still an active writer, lives in Santa Fe, New Mexico.

[2] On 23 June 1898 Gissing received a letter from Gabrielle Fleury (1869–1954) who asked permission to translate *New Grub Street* into French; and on July 6, while Gissing was visiting the Wellses, she called in person. Within a few days he was helping her with the translation in which he suggested cuts which amount to almost one-fourth of the English text. Gissing's response to Mlle Fleury must have been direct and immediate, for on July 10 he began *The Crown of Life*—that is, love.

46

GISSING TO WELLS

30 *July* 1898 7 *Clifton Terrace, Dorking*

MY DEAR H. G., I am glad to think of you in the life-giving air.[1] But even here it is tolerable just now, owing to the cool northern breeze.

Many thanks for writing to Hersey. I am eager for the new machine; this old one is very creaky and shaky. I have got so much at ease on wheels that I don't fear the change. I hope to heaven Hersey will be quick.

I am not sorry that Mrs Williams has come to Holmwood.[2] She is not at all likely to interfere with my working hours, and at other times I am glad to be saved from melancholy madness. She is a good and sensible and honest woman; I like her better the more I know her, and respect her not a little. Her weaknesses are amiable—a great thing. And, as I begin to see, she has a quite unusual loyalty and right feeling in her friendships.

My boy Walter arrived at Romney yesterday. No further news from the unspeakable quarter.

[1] The Wellses spent July at Lewes and August at Romney.

[2] In an undated letter to Mrs Wells from North Holmwood, Dorking, Mrs Williams wrote, "I have seen Mr Gissing once or twice. He came to lunch and spent the day with us Sunday. . . . I am so glad he likes to come here as I feel that if one could in any way make his life a little happier it would be a great thing."

The blackguard *Cosmopolis* has paid its debt.[1]

I have a delightful and wonderful letter from Mlle Fleury, on her return to Paris. The thing could be printed, so admirably is it phrased and shaped. And what a contrast to the letters, long and cumbersome, which I often receive from the typical Englishwoman who knows me through my books! Mlle Fleury has a mind of rare delicacy, emotional without emotionalism, sensitive to every appeal of art, and rich in womanly perceptiveness.[2] I am delighted to have made friends with her. She is the very best kind of Frenchwoman, uniting their fine intellectuality with the domestic sense which it is so common to think peculiarly English. She will very likely be in England again in October (after a Swiss holiday); if so, I shall rejoice.

Kindest remembrances to Mrs Wells (for all that she despises me) and to you every good wish.

Always sincerely,

George Gissing

[1] In 1898 *Cosmopolis: An International Monthly* published four Gissing short stories, his only stories for that year. The fact that *Cosmopolis* suspended publication with the issue of November 1898 suggests financial difficulty.

[2] Morley Roberts described Gabrielle Fleury with such terms as "high education," "extreme Gallic intelligence," and "very beautiful". (*The Private Life of Henry Maitland*, pp. 178–179.) Wells, however, appraised her quite differently and probably unfairly. Writing to Roberts in 1914 he declared, "Your estimate of Gabrielle is ridiculous. She was a tiresome weak sentimental middle-class Frenchwoman who wrote her letters on thin paper." (Letter to Roberts, *c.* 5 November 1914, Berg Collection.)

47

GISSING TO WELLS

15 *August* 1898 7 *Clifton Terrace, Dorking*

MY DEAR H. G., This is bad news which I receive from Hick.[1] I am very glad indeed that you went straight to him; I am sure he will devote himself to the care of you. My dear old boy, keep up heart of grace. This tropical weather must be very trying to you; me it has completely floored. But it won't last long; there will be chill blasts in a few days, depend upon it. How I wish I could come and sit by your bedside, and talk of follies to cheer you.—In truth, I might tell you of something more serious, but that shall be put off yet awhile. Some day there will be good news for you about my idiot self—news unexpected and inspiriting.[2] To me one of the happy features of the story is that it is connected with Worcester Park.

I am trying to write my Dickens prefaces.[3] A hard

[1] Wells had just suffered a serious and painful recurrence of his kidney ailment and had gone to Romney to consult Dr Henry Hick. He remained in Kent for a month, convalescing under Hick's care. (*Experiment in Autobiography*, VIII, 4.)

[2] Clearly Gissing recognised that his feeling for Mlle Fleury was serious and durable.

[3] Early in the summer Gissing had agreed to provide Methuen with introductions for a projected edition of Dickens. He began the work on August 10, probably after his vain attempts to begin *The Crown of Life*, and in the next two years wrote prefaces for twelve books—*Pickwick Papers*, *Sketches by Boz*, *Oliver Twist*, *Nicholas*

struggle. But the atmosphere is clearing. If only I could put that poor little child in safety, I should pluck up courage once more.

You will have seen the boy Walter. I want him to think of you as one of his friends; it will give him a decent subject of pride when he gets to the dangerous age.

Please tell H. H. that I am much bound to him for his letter, and will write very soon.

To Mrs Wells my kindest remembrances. I know how bravely and helpfully she will go through this time of stress.

Yours always heartily,

GEORGE GISSING

48

GISSING TO MRS WELLS

18 *August* 1898 7 *Clifton Terrace, Dorking*

MY DEAR MRS WELLS, I am moved more than I can tell you by the report of H. G.s condition. I had not pictured it to myself as so serious; indeed, I should otherwise

Nickleby, *Martin Chuzzlewit*, *Dombey and Son*, *Barnaby Rudge*, *The Old Curiosity Shop*, *Bleak House*, *David Copperfield*, *Christmas Books*, and *Master Humphrey's Clock*. Only the first nine of these were ever published, since the edition was abandoned in 1901. (Gordan, *George Gissing*, pp. 34–35.)

have written to him quite differently. Hick, out of good motive no doubt, minimised the trouble, and I thought of the dear old fellow as already risen from bed.—But we are not going to be gloomy, after all. He had strength of constitution to throw off that old lung mischief, and I hope right earnestly that his natural vigour will again assert itself.

Do say to him from me all possible kind and encouraging things. I regard H. G. as the friend of a lifetime; I can't do without him; he *must* be his old self again. My debt to his kindness, his good humour, his wit, is infinite. No, no; there shall be no talk about farewell to cycling. Some day, please heaven, he and I will ride about the English lanes again, and laugh over the dark things gone by.

You are very fortunate in having the help of such a trustworthy servant. I feel sure the Hicks will do their utmost; they are both good-natured Yorkshire folk, and in Hick's capacity as surgeon I have really good faith.

I shall not urge you to bear up through it all; *you* have no need of such idle phrases. In the last letter I had from him, H. G. spoke of you as the "unfailing chum," and he could have no better nurse beside him. But it is safe to bid you be careful of your own health—on all accounts.

Yes, of course I would think of the house at W. P., if anyone spoke to me on such a subject. You will have no trouble in letting it I feel sure.[1] I grieve that you have lived there so long.

You speak of Mrs Williams. She had a nasty accident on Holmwood Common the other day—being *knocked down* by a cricket ball! No bad results, happily. Lots of people come to see her, and I think she enjoys herself. It would not surprise me (this of course in all confidence) if we heard presently of her being about to marry again; I conjecture the likelihood from certain hints and appearances.

You delight me with your description of Walter. If only the other little boy could be with him! I can get no news now about the state of things in London, but it is pretty certain that the child's life is endangered whilst he remains with that madwoman. I told H. G.—did I not?—that she attacked her landlady with a stick, and was taken from the house with help of a policeman? She is now in I know not what lodgings.[2]

I have my mother staying with me here for a month.

Early in October comes Mlle Fleury, on a visit, after her return from Switzerland. You remember her? She has several times spoken of you.

Pray, do not think it necessary to reply to this or any

[1] Hick advised Wells to give up his home in Worcester Park and live in a dry air on sand and gravel. The Wellses had lived in Heatherlea somewhat less than two years.

[2] For the worsening of Mrs Gissing's state of mind and conduct see Gordan, *George Gissing*, p. 36. She died in February 1917 of an organic brain disorder.

other letter of mine. I want an occasional postcard, about H. G. You are *not* to weary yourself with letter-writing.

Affectionate regards to both of you. In a few days I shall send H. G. my vulgar new book,[1] for reading in convalescence.

Always yours,
GEORGE GISSING

49

GISSING TO WELLS

20 *August* 1898 7 *Clifton Terrace, Dorking*

MY DEAR H. G., It rejoices my heart to see your handwriting again. You send right good news; now steady onwards, and bate no jot of hope!

That you have to leave W. P. does not grieve me—much as I love the place; you had no right to be living on that low clay. Never mind, it is a memory, and for me a memory of the dearest. Some day I will explain to you all it means in the retrospect.

Hick has done bravely. I am very glad indeed you get on so well with him.

The *Chronicle* of to-day mentions your illness, as you

[1] *The Town Traveller* was published by Methuen on August 29. Originally intending it for serialisation Gissing had brightened the plot and treated his characters in a tone of amusement tinged with some condescension.

probably know. I had not heard of the foot-ball accident: years ago, I suppose.[1]—In the same column we are told that Morley Roberts is sailing for the Cape. He is going alone, and how the devil a man who is decently married can wander alone for half a year is beyond my comprehension. Such experiences should be left to the socially damned.

I am toiling at my Dickens prefaces—not easy things to do. Of course the heat makes any kind of work difficult: but this *prefacing* is no joke.—My ignoble novel comes out at the end of the month.

I have a book in mind—you remember my lurid hints of it. The only book I can hope to write just now is one which will help me—by its subject—through a time of torment.[2] Possibly it will give offence to the multitude—indeed I hope so.

I have had my new bicycle for 3 weeks. An excellent machine. It is already paid for. Hersey was very complying in the matter of proof-corrections—I mean, alterations of the bar, saddle, etc. But it is too hot to ride much nowadays.

My mother is here on a visit from Wakefield, for a month. Strange companions, she and I—with sadly

[1] In *Experiment in Autobiography*, VI, 1, Wells recalled his injury on the playing field of Holt Academy in Wrexham where he was a teacher.

[2] Gissing probably refers to his love for Mlle Fleury and *The Crown of Life*; but he seems not to have made any progress on the novel until October. (Gordan, *George Gissing*, p. 36.)

little to say to each other. My tumultuous mood does not make the situation easier.

No water in Dorking. Blackguard water-company drawing its 10%, and giving no supply!

I am tortured with eczema, as for some weeks past. Doctor coming frequently. Bill, at Christmas, £25, beyond a doubt.

When I come to fetch away Walter, I hope I shall see you. But you may be gone to Rye, by then.

All good be with you, old friend. Kindest regards to your wife.

Yours ever,
GEORGE GISSING

50

GISSING TO WELLS

26 *August* 1898 7 *Clifton Terrace, Dorking*

MY DEAR WELLS, I am glad indeed to hear that you have risen from bed; may you now quickly recover strength and flesh! Of course you have been dreadfully pulled down; but perhaps you have got rid of some internal enemy, and will live securely henceforth.

When you write again (not specially) will you let me know Hornung's address.[1] I want to ask him something about Australia—a point for use in fiction.

[1] Ernest William Hornung (1866–1921), brother-in-law of Conan Doyle, was another of the persons whom Gissing and Wells met in Rome. (Mrs Wells's diary records six visits with the

I shall send you a copy of *The Town Traveller*, but, if you dislike it, (as may very well be the case,) just leave it aside, and say nothing. It is a thin book; I couldn't help it.

The great heat is over; the autumnal mists begin to float about over meadows here, and no doubt the cold winds will very soon be blowing. Well, it generally means ability to work.

The Omar dinner is at Marlow on Sept 3. This time I shall not go.

I hope you may succeed quickly in finding a good house. I suppose you are well advised about the climatic conditions of Rye and Winchelsea. Rye, I should have thought a trifle damp; but I speak only from a glimpse of the place, and may be quite wrong.

My Dickens prefaces are occupying me. Not unpleasant work, but slow and anxious.

If only with a card, let me know of the stages of your convalescence.

With very kind regards to Mrs Wells,

Always yours,

GEORGE GISSING

Hornungs.) During the summer Hornung spent some time in England; and on July 3, just before departing for Naples, he wrote to Wells, "Give my love to dear old Gissing when you see or write to him, and tell him that he too ought to come and quaff the juice of Gaila grapes." Hornung had spent two years (1884–86) in Australia. If Gissing did make use of Australia in a novel after 1898, it has escaped the editor's search. In 1899 Hornung published *The Amateur Cracksman*, which introduced the celebrated Raffles.

51

GISSING TO WELLS

27 *August* 1898 7 *Clifton Terrace, Dorking*

Well, my dear boy, this is candour with a vengeance.[1] But you are too severe. My error has been in bearing so long with a woman who has used me so unmercifully. Of course I did it for the children's sake. And remember that, if I gave her the opportunity of getting a divorce, (an opportunity she would not use) I should incur the risk of having the children removed from my control. To them is my first responsibility, and I shall always recognize it.

Don't misinterpret me so harshly. I did not think your criticism of my view of life went so far; I ought to have kept silence about these things.

And, bythebye, it just occurs to me that perhaps you think I am referring to Mrs Williams! No, no, no. In that case my mysteriousness would be an injury to a person who has nothing to do with the matter.

I myself am absolutely free from moral obligations to

[1] The cause of Wells's outburst is not clear, but it may have been a letter from Gissing which has disappeared. That seems to be implied by a statement in Wells's letter (4 January 1904) to Edmund Gosse. In explaining the attachment between Gissing and Mlle Fleury, Wells wrote, "I remember the violent rage into which a sudden unbecoming sentimentality in Gissing's letters threw me—at that time."

the woman I married. (You would admit it if you knew her—or even if you spoke with impartial people who do.) And the woman to whom I foolishly alluded is free from obligations to anyone at all.

Far less energy of reproof would have stopped my mouth on such matters. Why were you so vehement?

Yours,
GEORGE GISSING

Why shouldn't I speak plainly?[1] It is Mlle Fleury, and if your life had been as lonely as mine, you would think very differently about one's relations with such a woman—relations innocent enough (in the conventional sense) and likely to remain so.

[1] It is puzzling that Gissing should have withheld Mlle Fleury's name until now, and it is difficult to believe that Wells did not surmise it. Early in October Gabrielle spent a week in Gissing's house under what Wells, in his letter to Gosse, described as "circumstances of extreme decorum—his mother was in the home with him at the time." This statement, however, does not square with Gissing's in Letter 36. And Gabrielle, in a letter of 10 June 1901 to Mrs Wells, declared that Gissing's mother and sisters did not even then know of her existence. On the other hand, Ellen Gissing, writing to Wells on 30 December 1903, expressed sympathy for Gabrielle and explained, "George himself told us all about her of course long ago, and as they both undertook it in a grave and serious spirit, and thought differently from us, we tried not to express our own deep-seated principles in a way that would be harsh or grieving to them." On October 15 Gissing noted in his diary that he and Gabrielle would live together in the spring, and on 7 May 1899 they were united in some kind of ceremony in Rouen. Wells explained to Gosse, "There was of course no marriage but everyone she [Gabrielle] knew in Paris, except her mother, thought it was a marriage."

52

GISSING TO WELLS

1 *September* 1898 7 *Clifton Terrace, Dorking*

My dear Wells, Let there be profoundest silence about a certain matter. I *knew* how it was, and had scarcely read that letter before I destroyed it. Please heaven it will soon pass altogether from my mind.

Of course I am glad you find *The Traveller* amusing. Bythebye, I have been so unlucky as to use the title "Bolsover"—which is actually existing. Yet I always make inquiry about such matters, and this time my authorities failed me.

This cool clear weather will favour your convalescence. You do not mention whether the house-hunting had any result. Be very careful about damp, etc., when you *do* go into a new abode. But I am in good hope of hearing before long that this bout has done you good rather than the reverse; you may find yourself free from bodily ailments for a long time to come.

Have you seen anything about Tolstoi's book on *Art*?[1] It is very interesting, but, to my mind, largely mistaken. He maintains that the untaught multitudes are

[1] *What is Art?* was published in 1898 and translated into English the same year. However Gissing read the French translation. (Jacob Korg, "Division of Purpose in George Gissing," *Publications of the Modern Language Association*, June 1955, 329.)

the sound judges of great art—citing the Old Testament stories as examples. But it is quite certain that even Biblical narratives are more fully appreciated by the cultivated than by the ignorant. He is in a confusion as to the meaning of the word "simple." Simple folk (in the high sense) do not belong to any particular class, and are found just as often among the rich as among the poor.

Bythebye, having to review the history of aesthetics, he never once mentions the name of Ruskin! Yet his theory of the moral significance of art is pure Ruskin.—Our friend Grant Allen comes in among the authorities.[1]

I shall soon hear that you are walking about the lanes. I hope the fine weather will last a little while yet. All good be with you!

Yours ever,
GEORGE GISSING

53

GISSING TO WELLS

28 *September* 1898 7 *Clifton Terrace*, *Dorking*

MY DEAR WELLS, I am anxious to hear whether you have come to a decision about the house. Are you still at Romney? And how are you feeling?

[1] Although Grant Allen (1848–99) had written a number of books on scientific subjects, he was after 1883 better known for his light novels and his travel books. His *Physiological Aesthetics* appeared in 1877 and may have been unknown to Gissing.

The change of weather is agreeable, but already one begins to ask how hands and feet are to be kept warm whilst desk-work is done. It has always been the winter problem with me. The ideal thing would be a little iron table, which could be placed immediately in front of the fire—if necessary, with legs in the fender. I have never yet found the room which could be warmed throughout by an ordinary fire.[1]

I have heard from Hornung. He says that nothing more than a week's discomfort resulted from his accident. They stay through the winter at Posilippo.

A marvelous late-summer this! Day after day, here, without a cloud in the sky. I have been getting up warm curtains, carpets, etc., preparing for the winter campaign.

Please to remember that henceforth I have a spare bedroom here, and that if you and Mrs Wells ever feel able to spend a day or two in these parts you will rejoice me by taking possession.

Kindest regards to both of you, and, if you are still at Romney, remembrances to all the Hick household.

Always yours,

GEORGE GISSING

[1] Yet in *The Private Papers of Henry Ryecroft*, "Winter," I, Gissing wrote, "If my room were kept warm by some wretched modern contrivance of water pipes or heated air, would it be the same to me as that beautiful core of glowing fuel, which, if I sit and gaze into it, becomes a world of wonders?"

54

GISSING TO WELLS

16 *October* 1898 7 *Clifton Terrace, Dorking*

MY DEAR H. G., Many thanks for your good note, which I am too late in answering. I think you have done very wisely. You will be able to test the climate before comitting yourself.[1] May all go well with you!

Work has me by the throat. If I fulfil my purpose, I shall be here in rigid seclusion (save for the Omar dinner) for the next three months.[2] We must exchange news, of course.

Always kindest regards to your wife. And believe me

Ever yours,
G. G.

[1] Wells had decided to live for a time in rented quarters at Sandgate near Folkestone.

[2] Gissing's new determination to work on *The Crown of Life* was probably due to the fact that on the preceding day he and Gabrielle had decided to cast their lot together.

55

GISSING TO WELLS

6 November 1898 *7 Clifton Terrace, Dorking*

MY DEAR WELLS, Yes it is industry—industry and eczema. The latter, I fear, is due to some local conditions; it drives me mad, and I see little chance of getting rid of it. None the less, I am working steadily, and shall do so—please heaven—without a break to Christmas.

If you could remember, you might just ask H. H. whether he holds the theory that eczema is merely a skin disease, and not relative to state of blood. A London doctor says I may eat what I like—it matters nothing. But I have grave doubts.

Capital news, about your house.[1] I had no idea that Mrs Hick's brother was an architect. Well, you will at all events be able to lay down the law in the matter of this edifice, if never again.

Evans was here for a night on Tuesday—on his way to stay with his gorgeous relatives at Wardour Castle.[2]

[1] Wells engaged C. A. F. Voysey, one of the first architects to rebel against Victorian ornateness, to design and construct a home at Sandgate. (*Experiment in Autobiography*, VIII, 6.)

[2] Wardour Castle was the seat of the Arundels, a Roman Catholic family famous in Elizabethan times. W. M. Evans was on the staff of the *Monitor*, a Roman Catholic weekly, and he later became secretary of Newman House. Gissing's appraisal of him is reflected in a statement from Evans's letter of 22 August 1898 to

He is entering upon journalism, and *may* hold his own. A good fellow.—Then, I have a copy of the *Baltimore Sun*, containing a descriptive article by Brian O'Dunne—rather good.[1] He, the excellent Brian, will undoubtedly make a journalist.

Apropos whereof, a man writes to me from *Sewanee* (Tennessee), drawing my attention to an enthusiastic article of his on my immortal works in the *Sewanee Review*.[2] This is fame.

So the novel is finished; good.[3] You are evidently in right-working trim, and it rejoices me to know it. All your arrangements have been happily contrived; but then, with the exception of this late floorer, you have a tradition of prosperous circumstance. And may it long hold good!

This morning (Sunday) I am about to set forth for a bicycle ride. Ockley way. I have had but little of it

---

Mrs Wells, " Gissing wrote me a charming letter exhorting me as far as I could gather to lead a 'placid life' and to try and conquer any feeling that I must be 'doing something' to be useful in life." Gissing studied the type in Henry Ryecroft and Lord Dymchurch, a character in *Our Friend the Charlatan.*

[1] This was an account of a visit to Gibraltar.

[2] "A Novelist of the Hour," *Sewanee Review* (July 1898) by Greenough White was actually an extended review of *The Whirlpool.* It developed the thesis that this novel was "modern"—by reason of its subject-matter, lack of humour, and remorseless analysis of character.

[3] *When the Sleeper Wakes*, published in May 1899 after serialisation in the *Graphic*.

lately. Beyond doubt the summer of riding did me physical good—spite of the thrice-accursed eczema.

John Davidson has sent me his new play. Alas! I *try* to like it.[1]

I saw the announcement of Munthe's volume, and wish I could see the book itself.[2] At your house I read a story of Conrad's, with interest.[3]

Harold Frederic! Appalling business.[4] That poor silly woman has got into hideous complications. Of

[1] Gissing had taken John Davidson (1857–1909) as guest to the Omar dinner (20 November 1896) at which he first met Wells. Though best known for his *Fleet Street Eclogues* Davidson began his literary career by writing plays. The one here referred to, *Godfrida* (1898), was praised by Max Beerbohm in the *Saturday Review* (29 October 1898).

[2] Axel Munthe (1857–1949), the Swedish psychiatrist, began reminiscing in *Vagaries* (1898).

[3] Wells, one of the first enthusiasts for Conrad, had praised *Almayer's Folly* and *An Outcast of the Islands* in the *Saturday Review* (16 May 1896). The story Gissing here alludes to may have been *The Nigger of the "Narcissus"* or one of the *Tales of Unrest*. Gissing shared Wells's enthusiasm. After reading *Youth*, he wrote, "No man at present writing fiction has such a grip at reality, such imaginative vigour, and such wonderful command of language, as Joseph Conrad." (Clodd, *Memories*, p. 186.)

[4] Frederic died on October 19 under circumstances which led a coroner's jury to bring a charge of manslaughter against Kate Lyon and Mrs Mills. They were Christian Scientists and were allegedly responsible for Frederic's rejection of medical aid: hence Gissing's reference to Portland prison. The Crown acquitted them and found that Frederic's obstinacy was a sufficient explanation of his refusal to obey doctors' orders. For Kate Lyon, "that poor silly woman," see Letters 57–58. The novel, *Gloria Mundi*, was published November 1898. Gissing became acquainted with Frederic at an Omar Khayyám dinner on 20 June 1896.

course Mrs Mills should be sent at once to Portland.—And the poor fellow's novel, by all accounts, seems to be magnificent.

What about *Aylwin*?[1] I have a rooted suspicion (not having seen the book) that it is the most flagrant case of (not quite explicable) log-rolling known in our time. It puzzles me. Quotations read very poorly indeed, and the man I know to be a pretentious bore. But *why* does every critic grovel at his feet? Is it simply because, for thirty years, he has worried the privacy of Swinburne?

Mrs Wells, I hope and doubt not, is in good health. My kindest remembrances to her.

Ever yours,
GEORGE GISSING

[1] Gissing must have read the review of Theodore Watts-Dunton's *Aylwyn* in the *Athenaeum* (22 October 1898). The five columns of fulsome praise, together with the spacious advertisement preceding it, were a piece of puffery equal to the brazen panegyrics of Colburn in the heyday of puffing. The review made use of familiar tactics: the reminder that *Aylwyn* had been long withheld from the public, hints about "persons" who had "influenced" the story, and the inevitable conclusion that *Aylwyn* was more than literature—it was life. One simple explanation for the log-rolling was that Watts-Dunton was at this time the principal critic on the *Athenaeum*.

56

GISSING TO WELLS

9 *December* 1898 7 *Clifton Terrace, Dorking*

MY DEAR WELLS, As you know, a time of toil is without news. I have had nothing to tell, and it was useless to lament my bodily ills.

Pinker told me that you were worried about the building. I suppose no man ever yet built without worries endless, but you should not undertake much of the business yourself. Your time is too valuable.

I have pictured Beach Cottage rocking in gales and lashed with furious rain.[1] I'll warrant you have enough fresh air just now. Heaven be thanked, the sun shows a little at last!

I have heard once or twice from O'Dunne. He has made a beginning of journalism at Baltimore, and writes with all the glee of a youth in such case. He finds your books abundantly read in Baltimore, and, I can see, chuckles over his ability to declare acquaintance with the author. From the samples of his journalism which he has sent (sketches of his life in Europe) I have no doubt he will do well enough.

[1] Beach Cottage, to which Wells moved after his convalescence in Romney, was a small house near the sea at Sandgate. In rough weather the waves broke over the roof, and the Wellses pushed forward their plans to build a new home.

How do you get on in health? Hick, I suppose, regularly sees you still?—The invasion of friends at all hours is a very serious matter; happily, the bad weather will give you a short respite. For my own part, I have never yet understood how a literary man with many people anxious to see him, and allowing his address to be commonly known, ever did any work at all. True, I see all the difficulty of living in any other way. It is the curse of the literary calling.

I see no new books—except one or two which their authors are good enough to send me. I like what was quoted in the reviews of Newbolt's new volume.[1] Jingoism is abhorrent to me, and I wish the man had written on any other subject; but he undoubtedly writes poetry, and some of it admirable.

I go nowhere. The Omar dinner must be attended, I suppose, on the 16th, but I wish it were not held in that pestilent city—every day more a subject of loathing to me.

The brave Pinker is taking some of my affairs in hand, and you shall know the results of his activity some day.[2]

[1] Henry Newbolt's volumes of ballads and marching songs, *Admirals All* (1897) and *The Island Race* (1898), were immensely popular. Such poems as "The Death of Admiral Blake," "Drake's Drum," and "San Stefano" chimed with the popular feeling aroused by the Kaiser's announced policy of strengthening the German army.

[2] In arranging for the publication of *The Crown of Life* Gissing called upon the services of Pinker, who secured £300 from Methuen—that is, £50 more than the firm had paid for *The Town Traveller*—and also £100 from F. A. Stokes. (Gordan, *George Gissing*, p. 37.)

Mrs Wells is well, I hope. Pray remember me very kindly to her.

Always yours,
GEORGE GISSING

57

GISSING TO WELLS

2 *January* 1899 7 *Clifton Terrace, Dorking*

MY DEAR WELLS, Hearty thanks for your long and delightful letter. And hearty good wishes to you for the New Year! With native brutality I did not reply to your card (just as tasteful as card can be—really good) but I am so overwhelmed with toil; I answered in thought, be sure.

The house worry must be maddening. Dare you really begin it all over again? Well, you are courageous. And those visitors! I fall sick with terror in thinking of them. If by rare chance anyone comes here, it means to me the loss of a whole day, a most serious matter.

But the news of your health is really excellent. It does me good to know you so much better.

I am drawing to the end of a long novel which the brave Pinker will sell for me. I want money sorely. It is an Anti-jingo book.[1]

On the list of subscribers to the Frederic fund, I saw

[1] In *The Crown of Life* Gissing repeatedly inveighed against the rising jingoism, which was largely due to the increasing threat of Russia in the Orient and to the Kaiser's determination to enlarge the German navy as well as the army.

you down for £5. I fear this represents your final gift in that direction. Yet the fact is that Kate Lyon and her three little children (the eldest seven years old) are in far more serious need than Mrs Frederic and her two grown up daughters and two boys of 10 and 12.[1] They have the brute world against them—and it has shown its bestiality in ways that make me rage up and down the room. Of course no public subscription can be opened for them, but certain people are doing their best, especially Mrs Stephen Crane and the executor Stokes. The children are away in the country, in good hands, and we want to secure them there for a year or two, till it can be seen what Kate Lyon can do. Of course their identity has to be concealed—else the sweet neighbours would make life impossible for the people who take care of them.

Grrrr!!

How I should have liked to share in the awful haggis! If you ever write to the Perth ladies, will you say how gladly I remember them.

Yes, I hope to see you some day. All good be with you.

Always yours,[2]

[1] Harold Frederic left two families—his legitimate one and another by Kate Lyon to whom he became attached in 1889. Both were in need of funds, for Frederic was always hard pressed for money. Mrs Crane was concerned because her husband, upon his arrival in England in 1897, formed a close friendship with Frederic. John Stokes was Frederic's secretary. (Paul Haines, *Harold Frederic*, unpublished dissertation, New York University, 1945.)

[2] The signature is missing.

58

GISSING TO WELLS

3 *January* 1899 7 *Clifton Terrace*, *Dorking*

MY DEAR WELLS, It's an odd thing that your subscription so miscarried. Harris is said to have been very loyal in the weaker side; at present, I think, he is abroad, and presumably doing nothing particular. Perhaps he left England before your cheque arrived. Could anyone else have opened the letter?[1]

There is as yet no printed list, and Mrs Stephen Crane has not yet persuaded her bankers to hold the fund. *She* must be a brick. She had the three little ones for four months, at her own house, during H. F's illness, and seems, together with Stokes, to have kept the poor woman alive through all the horrors. Mrs Crane's address is Ravensbrook, Oxted, Surrey, and she will joyfully answer any question. It is Stokes's hope that a very rich man named Lawrence, who lives at Kenley, a friend of H. F's, will do something solid for the children, and that another rich man named Barry (after whom the youngest is named) will also help substantially.[2] But rich men are slow.

[1] Does this mean that Frank Harris, who was capable of dark deeds, misappropriated Wells's contribution to the Frederic fund?

[2] Sir Joseph Lawrence (1848–1919) was president of the British Linotype Company. Barry has eluded identification.

I seriously doubt whether you ought to give another £5. Indeed, I am sure you ought *not*—quite sure. I wish I had not shared my stupid 4 guineas between the two—but when I decided to do that I had heard only Fisher's story, not Stokes's.[1] Stokes abuses no one; he is a fair man, and says Fisher speaks in honest ignorance.

In any case, you ought certainly to communicate with Mrs Crane before sending any money. I am waiting to hear that the thing has been put in order at the bankers'.

You have pleased me by writing in this way—but of course I knew that you hadn't heard all the facts.

Ah, the building! I wish you were out of it.

Always yours,
GEORGE GISSING

59

GISSING TO WELLS [postcard]

3 *January* 1899 *Dorking*

I forgot about the interview. It was done very faithfully in my case. You simply dictate to the man, who is helpless and without original ideas about anything.

G. G.

[1] J. G. Fisher, a member of the Savage Club, supported Frederic's bid for membership in 1884.

60

GISSING TO WELLS

28 *March* 1899 *Dorking*

MY DEAR WELLS, I reply to your welcome note as well as shakiness will allow. It is 6 weeks since I left the house. Influenza, followed by pleurisy and all sorts of things. Never in my life have I had so long an illness. Of course I am beginning to pay the penalty of many years of insufficient food and every kind of unhealthiness; it is a rather serious breakdown.

You, I gather, are very well, and I rejoice to think of you as settling in a comfortable house.[1] Never mind about the building; it is a hideous business.

I shall try to see you before I go abroad, but it is plain that I have seriously to economise strength.

This is not a letter. I will write very soon. The S.W. wind affects me just like the scirocco.

Kindest remembrances to you both.

Ever yours,
GEORGE GISSING

[1] The Wellses had just moved to Arnold House, Sandgate.

61

GISSING TO WELLS

21 *April* 1899 7 *Clifton Terrace*, *Dorking*

MY DEAR WELLS, From amid wreck and ruin—that is to say the unutterable misery of removal—I write you and your wife a good-bye word. To-morrow I go down into Worcestershire for a few days—my boy Walter is there just now—then out into the world once more.[1]

A hideous thing has marked to-day. You must know that I had chosen and packed with great care some fifty volumes, to be presently sent to me abroad; well, in the transit to the warehouse, the box *broke*, and—but it is too loathsome to talk of. I have been perspiring, gasping, coughing, and trembling all day long. Two more such days, and I should move into my grave.

My dear fellow, no common phrase of thanks will answer your offer about money. It was finely generous, but I should be very hard driven indeed before I seized, even for a time, upon that blessed hoard of yours. Great heavens! A literary man able to declare that he has hundreds laid aside![2] It is too wonderful for envy.

[1] Gissing was preparing to go to France to join Gabrielle.

[2] In *Experiment in Autobiography*, VIII, 6, Wells remarked that at this time he had all the money needed to build Spade House and a surplus of more than £1000.

I am going to write—or try to write—my sixth-century story, and hope to have done it by the end of this year. All is planned out—even the names selected, and the opening seen pretty clearly.[1] This change will, I dare say, rest my mind. Meredith warns me very gravely of the public disinclination to take a new thing from an old man, but for the rest is pleased with the idea.[2] I have got into such a loathing of the present world that I *could* not write about it just now.

It is a pity (perhaps a calamity) that my finished novel could not appear this spring.[3] But publishers will take their own course, and on the whole they seem to know less about publishing than any order of men.

I had a good account of you from Pinker last Sunday.

[1] According to his diary Gissing had worked out his historical novel in June 1897. Even now he apparently did not begin to write it. Probably because of the need for money he felt obliged to produce a book quickly, and his next work was *By the Ionian Sea*, written between 28 June and 9 August 1899. On 26 October 1900, three days after he finished *The Private Papers of Henry Ryecroft*, he once more began to think over the Roman novel, but he did not begin the writing until Christmas Day. (*Letters of George Gissing to His Family*, p. 351, and Gordan, *George Gissing*, p. 41.)

[2] Meredith kept up his interest in Gissing's life and career. In 1902 he wrote a kind letter and asked Gissing for "some account" of himself. (Clodd, *Memories*, p. 181.)

[3] The delay in the negotiations for the sale of *The Crown of Life* was probably due to Pinker's desire to get the best possible price for it. Writing to Wells on 24 June 1902 Pinker explained that he had always had to sell Gissing's work in such a hurry that there was "no chance for terms." *The Crown of Life* was published in October 1899.

I am really glad to hear of your comfortable settlement. Some day I shall see you, I hope.

An American interviewer came here to see me the other day. She writes that she is soon going "*accross*" again. Merciful powers! What a time we live in!

You shall hear of me soon. Kindest remembrances to both of you.

Ever yours cordially,
GEORGE GISSING

62

GISSING TO WELLS [postcard]

3 *May* 1900 *Paris*

On returning, I was seized with an attack of intercostal rhumatism, and am still in bed.[1] Very glad to have your letter. Pray let me know, as soon as you can, the *date* of your arrival at Paris. I find that rooms have everywhere to be taken considerably in advance; the crush is growing serious.—You shall have the plan of the habitation as soon as I can leave the house.—With regard to Davray,[2]

[1] During April 2–30 Gissing was in England, where he visited his mother in Wakefield, the Clodds, and the Wellses. Gabrielle opposed the trip because she feared the effect on Gissing's health and also because she was anxious about his attachment to his family. See Letter 78.

[2] Presumably Wells thought that Davray might be of some service to Gissing. In the *Mercure de France* (May 1901) Davray praised *New Grub Street* and *Born in Exile* at some length and in the highest terms. The only fault he remarked in these novels was "*bien des pages où l'action traîne et s'attarde en d'inutiles dialogues.*"

I would gladly know him, but I fear the meeting may be a little difficult of arrangement, as you certainly will have no time to spare. Still, if we could manage it, the best way would be for us all to lunch together at some restaurant. In any case, I hope you and your brother will gratify me by lunching or dining with me somewhere on one of the days.—But, if possible, let me have a precise *date*. Of course I would telegraph to S. Germain, but it is very improbable that rooms could be found at short notice. Kindest regards to you all.

G. G.

63

GISSING TO WELLS

23 *May* 1900 *Paris*

MY DEAR WELLS, The boisterous weather made me think uneasily of you on your return journey[1]—I hope you managed to do all that you had in mind, and without discomfort.

On Friday evening we leave for our summer quarters. Address:

Villa des Roses
St Honoré-les-bains
Nièvre
France.

[1] Wells had been on a cycling tour in France.

I hope and trust that there we shall remain until the middle of October, and that I shall do an honest bit of work.[1]

Pray don't lose the address, and let me hear from you before long. If you can send the photographs, so much the better.

Remember me very kindly to Mrs Wells, and believe me

Cordially yours,
GEORGE GISSING

A little chuckle of pleasure denotes my recollection now and then of our eating together in Paris. Your brother interested me.[2] I sympathized vigorously with his declaration against "Sunday labour."

[1] They stayed until the end of October, and Gissing's work went very well. On May 28 he made a fresh start on *Our Friend the Charlatan* (then called *The Coming Man*) which he had vainly begun on 29 September 1899. Two days later he wrote in his diary, "Better work, I think, than I have done since *New Grub Street*." (*Letters of George Gissing to His Family*, p. 370.)

[2] Francis Charles Wells (1857–1933) was an eccentric whose effervescence comes out in a letter to H. G. in which he vividly recalls the cycling tour. There is an interesting passage on Sunday in *The Private Papers of Henry Ryecroft*, "Summer," IV.

64

GISSING TO MRS WELLS

31 *May* 1900 *Villa des Roses, St Honoré-les-bains*

Dear Mrs Wells, Many thanks for your letter and the photographs. As regards these brown presentments, I suspect they are about the most faithful ever taken of me. That in which I turn to the heavens has incited protest; it is possible that I do not there show to advantage, looking rather like some contributor to *Ally Sloper*[1] in a heavily hilarious mood. But the others are acceptable to all concerned. Thank you for all the trouble you have taken.

I am pleased to have the excellent likeness of H. G., and to see you—though dimly—amid the rising walls of your house. These things will have historic value.

We are much at ease in this villa, amid a large garden full of flowers and fruit. St Honoré lies on the lowest undulations of the Morvan hills, which are magnificently wooded. One might easily imagine oneself in England;[2]

[1] Ally Sloper, an absurd cartoon figure created by W. G. Baxter, appeared regularly on the front page of *Ally Sloper's Half Holiday*, a comic weekly published 1884–1923.

[2] The longing of the expatriate now appears in Gissing's letters. On June 17 he wrote to his son, "It is wonderfully like England, and I see all the old flowers—foxgloves, honeysuckle, rockrose, yellow rattle and numberless more." (*Letters of George Gissing to His Family*, p. 370.)

there is very little "foreign" in the scene. The air seems splendid, and farm produce is abundant.

I am working steadily, glorying in the blessed country stillness after noisy Paris.

Kindest remembrances to you both.

Always yours,
GEORGE GISSING

65

GISSING TO WELLS

3 *July* 1900 *Villa des Roses, St Honoré-les-bains*

MY DEAR WELLS, I am late in writing to you about your book.[1] I myself was able to read it at once, but I wanted my wife to have read it also, that I might give her opinion with my own. We have both enjoyed it much.

It is very well done, very fresh and full of life. The impression left upon me as I closed the book was one of strong pathos. That struggle with dire poverty and youth's illusions! Your humorous method is responsible for much in the effect—in the originality of the whole thing. There is nothing not well seen—both by writer and reader, and many things very admirably realized by very simple means.

Gabrielle speaks with special delight of "Mr Chaffery

[1] *Love and Mr Lewisham*, published in June 1900.

at Home."[1] Mr Lagune is also a favourite of hers. These strike her as uncommonly good psychology, very amusingly presented.

Odd, how long ago it seems since I heard you say—speaking of this story—that you had just "got the young people married"![2]

How I wish it were possible for Mrs Wells and you to get as far as this place. Heaven be thanked, I am working peacefully and regularly.

Your house, meanwhile, is rising. I imagine it already visible on the hillside. I wonder whether I shall ever see it.

Hearty thanks for your kindness in sending the book, and kindest remembrances to you both from both of us.

Always yours,

GEORGE GISSING

[1] In this amusing chapter Lewisham is confronted by his step-father-in-law, who is a professional medium and a loquacious rogue. Mr Lagune is a spiritualist.

[2] In a letter of 30 July 1900 to Arnold Bennett, Wells remarked a similarity between *Love and Mr Lewisham* and Bennett's *A Man from the North*: "Your approach and line of thought are clearly rather more toward Gissing than are mine, and I am reminded by that, that Gissing some years ago when I was telling him the idea of *Lewisham* told me that he also had contemplated the same story. His title was to have been *The Common Lot*, and there you have as compactly as possible a certain difference in the point of view."

66

GISSING TO WELLS

14 *August* 1900 *Villa des Roses, St Honoré-les-bains*

MY DEAR WELLS, Thank you very much for the Italian translation of *The Invisible Man*. I have read it with enjoyment.

If you care to correct misprints, the word *esclamai*, near bottom of p. 64 should be *esclamo*. Also, *di sopra*, at bottom of p. 123 should be *di sotto*—for the breakfast was certainly not prepared in a room *above* the bedroom. There is also something curious at the top of p. 114. *Vedi questa macchia*, etc. "You see this spot? My blood becomes *invisible* when it coagulates." Surely *invisible* should be *visible*?

Very amusing, here and there, the Italian rendering of things familiar. Thus the *St James's Gazette* masks comically as the *Gazzeta di San Giacomo*. The translator has an evil habit about names of places, especially streets. On the same page he writes "Great Portland Street," and "la Strada di Great Portland." "La Collina di Primrose" invites mirth. But best of all in this way is "il Corsa di Tottenham"!

It rejoices me that you care for *The Ionian Sea*.

Chapman & Hall tell me they want to make a good illustrated volume of it.[1]

I hope Wyzcwa will soon do *Mr Lewisham* for the *Revue des Deux Mondes*.[2] It is a good book, and will excite much attention in France.

So your chimneys are already rising. I wish I could see them—aye, that I do!

Remember me to Mrs Wells, and believe me,

Always yours,

GEORGE GISSING

[1] Gissing completed *By the Ionian Sea* early in August 1899, but it was not until the following February that the book was sold—for 120 guineas—to the *Fortnightly Review*, where the first instalment appeared in May. In June Chapman & Hall bought a seven-year lease on the book for £130. The illustrations, done by Leo de Littrow from sketches by Gissing, delayed the publication of the book until June 1901.

[2] T. de Wyzewa did not review *Love and Mr Lewisham*. He did, however, make *Mr Britling Sees It Through* the subject of an extended essay in the *Revue des deux Mondes* of 15 November 1916.

67

WELLS TO GISSING[1]

19 *October* 1900 *Arnold House, Sandgate, Kent*

MY DEAR GISSING, The days slip by and there being no specific thing to write about there comes with none of them the now-or-never that stirs to the act of correspondence. Just where are we? Just as we were when you were with us—except that the *Fortnightly* will cease to interest me after this month.[2] I do really admire and delight in your *By the Ionian Sea* which seems not only to me but to almost all the people I hear speak of such things, by far the finest work you have done—in conception and quality alike. Popham that good man next door[3] gets the *Fortnightly* from me and after that Joseph Conrad bears it off and then it goes to Hick. And it

[1] This letter has an envelope which bears the address, "13 Rue de Siam; Passy, Paris." It was readdressed, "Poste Restante; Trient, Valais, Suisse." The letter was unclaimed and was returned to Wells.

[2] The last instalment of *By the Ionian Sea* appeared in the October issue of the *Fortnightly Review*.

[3] The Pophams were congenial neighbours to the Wellses when they lived in Arnold House. Mrs Popham's letters to Mrs Wells reveal her vibrant personality. In one of them (4 November 1902) she wrote, in reference to her book, *The Housewives of Edenrise*, "I have had a charming letter from Gissing to whom I sent a copy. He couldn't have said anything nasty of course but politeness did not demand anything so encouraging."

promises well for the book when it comes that James has just made a success with some French travel impressions.[1]

Our house is now very nearly done indeed and we hope in another month to be up there. The plumber draws near the end of his labours, the last grate was being fixed today, every day I get paint on my clothes from some pleasingly unexpected quarter, there is glass in the verandah door and the scraper has come. Also there is a man a planting trees. Up and down the pergola (which isn't a pergola at all that being merely its name) we have stuck 500 daffodils—or 800—there is room for a dispute how many there were in a bag, but anyhow a marvellous number.

Let us know how you are and when you are coming this way to England again. And if you should come why should not Madame Gissing come also—at least thus far into England—while you wander further into Pinkerdom and so forth?

And with our kindest regards to you both

Believe me ever my dear Gissing,

Yours most sincerely

H. G. WELLS

[1] Henry James's *A Little Tour in France* was published in October.

68

GISSING TO WELLS

27 *November* 1900 13 *Rue de Siam, Passy, Paris*

MY DEAR WELLS, I want to hear from you. Is the house finished?[1] When do you move in? What are you doing? I have come back from the country with a hunger for news; pray write. Somebody tells me that a novel of yours is to appear in the *Revue de Paris*.[2] Which? And when?

Please let me know Davray's address. I know it is Avenue d'Orléans, but have forgotten the number. I want to go to see him and invite him to come here.

I suspect things are very bad in England, and likely to be so for long enough.[3] You, perhaps, feel nothing of it; for my own part, I foresee the possibility of having to find some new way of earning a living, which, under the circumstances (indeed, under my circumstances) would be difficult enough.

Remember me very kindly to Mrs Wells. Do you ever see Hick? Above all, are you in health and spirits?

Ever yours,

GEORGE GISSING

[1] Spade House was completed in December 1900.

[2] *The Invisible Man*, translated by Achille Laurent, was serialised in the *Revue de Paris* 1 December 1900–15 January 1901.

[3] Parliament had been dissolved on September 17 on issues arising from the war in South Africa.

69

GISSING TO WELLS

13 *January* 1901 13 *Rue de Siam*, *Paris*

MY DEAR WELLS, Your letter is more than welcome. It contains many pieces of good news—the best, perhaps, that which promises your passing through Paris at the end of March. A flat, as you know, is not a human abode, and with difficulty we lodge ourselves here, with no corner to offer a friend, but I earnestly hope that we shall be able to see you at that time, somehow.

Nothing simpler than to come back by way of Lyons. You cross the Mt Cenis to Chambéry, and then change for the line which goes direct, via St André-le-Gaz, to Lyons. I will send you the *Indicateur* in two days. It comes out twice a month, and you must have the latest number.

Gabrielle protests against the idea that Avignon would disappoint you. In fine weather, I believe it is a most wonderful place—though it is true that the "County Council" has just destroyed one of the finest gates. Queer to think that such a dry stick as J. S. Mill made it his favourite abode.[1]

[1] On the dissolution of the East India Company in 1858 John Stuart Mill left England for Southern Europe. His wife became ill en route and died at Avignon, whereupon Mill bought a house overlooking the cemetery and spent six months of each year

I am very glad that Lucas thinks well of my new novel, but do not forget that Harpers *refused* it.[1] Be very moderate in your expectations. On the other hand, I have actually begun my 6th century story, and think I am making something of it. It must be finished this summer. Just now, I am in fearful disorder, for all my books have just arrived from their warehouse house at Dorking.

What is the meaning of the fact that this morning I receive two political letters, from strangers, one asking me to subscribe for the support of Keir Hardie,[2] the other (from Secretary of St Pancras Something Association) asking if I will stand for the L.C.C.? Is not the latter probably a joke? Or has someone been writing about my political genius—such an excellent subject for the journalist?

It rejoices me that your prospects are so bright. Owing

---

there. His spending one hour every day in the cemetery, his dedication of his essay *On Liberty* (1859) to his wife's memory and the epitaph he composed for her white marble tomb are evidence of greater depth of feeling than Gissing gave him credit for.

[1] E. V. Lucas was the English representative of Harper & Brothers of New York. Early in January the American rights of *Our Friend the Charlatan* were bought by Henry Holt for £150.

[2] James Keir Hardie (1856–1915) violently opposed the Boer War and thereby endangered his political future. However he was elected to Parliament in 1900 and formed the Labour Representative Committee which later became the Labour Party.

to the tone of Continental journalism,[1] I find myself thinking of England as hopelessly sunk in defeat and bankruptcy. Perhaps this is not really the state of things; you are better able to judge. I heartily wish it were possible for Gabrielle and me to come to Sandgate; but the weak health of Mme Fleury makes absence on G's part out of the question yet a while. But I assure you she is delighted with your very kind invitation, and hopes as much as I do that we shall see you both at the end of March.

Expect, then, the *Indicateur*.

Bythebye, have you heard from Davray? He promised to write to me from Capri, but every excuse is to be made for a man in that uncertain health.

Our kindest regards to Mrs Wells, who, I know, must be rejoicing in the beautiful new house. Well, well, if ever I am able to see you there, there will be a new member of the family[2]—one, I hope, whose life will look into a better time.

Ever yours,
GEORGE GISSING

[1] The hostility of the French press toward Great Britain was an expression of the tension that had developed from the Fashoda incident, the Dreyfus affair, and other points of friction.

[2] In *Experiment in Autobiography*, VIII, 6, Wells wrote, "The house was still being built when it dawned upon us as a novel and delightful idea that we were now justified in starting a family."

79

GISSING TO WELLS

6 *March* 1901 13 *Rue de Siam*, *Paris*

My dear Wells, Delighted to have your telegram. Yes, come on Friday at 7 o'clock.[1] We are on the second floor (second above ground-floor), the door on the *right* hand as you reach the landing. Knowing this, you need not worry with the offensive concierge.

Be careful in this terrible weather. We await you anxiously.

Yours ever,

G. G.

I have just received your letter, but of course I understand that the telegram is *the thing*. You say "I" can dine —of course you mean "*we*."

Friday, then, at 7—and both of you.

71

GISSING TO WELLS

12 *April* 1901 13 *Rue de Siam*, *Paris*

My dear Wells, The brave Hick has been writing to me and I have satisfied him that, for the present, I am

[1] After spending some weeks in Italy the Wellses stopped in Paris on their return journey. They were there on Friday, March 8.

going on fairly well. Early in June we go either to St Honoré or to Autun, and there I shall consider whether I can venture upon a trip to England in August. One *health* motive would be that in England I should put on flesh, which I never can here.[1] The other motives are numerous and strong. I want to see you all, and fear, positively fear, the next winter, if I have not this refreshment in between.

Many, many thanks for your letter—full of kindness as your letters always are. You shall hear when we are in the country.

All good things from us both to both of you. I hope Mrs Wells keeps strong and in spirits.

I hear there is a 6d edition of *Stolen Bacillus*.[2] You might some day post a copy.

Always yours,

GEORGE GISSING

[1] This sentence, together with a passage in the following letter, tends to bear out Morley Roberts's opinion that the deterioration in Gissing's health was due to under-nourishment. According to Roberts, Gissing wanted and needed fine fat feeding which was not provided by French cookery. Furthermore Gabrielle's invalid mother, who lived with the Gissings, had definite and exiguous notions about food, and she bitterly criticised the grossness of Gissing's taste when he wished for more substantial breakfasts. Although Roberts's pages on this question seem overwritten, he was in fact drawing upon Gissing's letters to him and upon Dr Hick who, in a letter (23 February 1904) to Wells, declared that "French starvation caused Gissing to go to pieces." (*The Private Life of Henry Maitland*, pp. 196 ff.)

[2] This book of stories was first published November 1895. The stories had originally appeared in the *Pall Mall Gazette* and other periodicals.

72

GABRIELLE GISSING TO MRS WELLS

[*April* 1901]

DEAR MRS WELLS, George wants me to make you aware that this time we must not joke about his health; things are becoming rather serious, most unfortunately! I don't know whether he told you he had got a bad cold at Wakefield the last time he went to England last spring, he did not tell me that till lately, so that though I saw him changing and getting thinner and thinner I could not guess exactly what was the cause of it. Things were so bad lately, he became so weak, unable to work, etc., that he consented at last to go and see a specialist, a very clever doctor, professor at the Faculté de Médecine here. And the result of the consultation is that, owing to the fact of his neglected cold of last spring his "pulmonary conditions" are very bad. He has got long prescriptions to do, burning points, etc.; the doctor says he ought to rest many months, which of course he will not do. But what makes George very sorry is that the Doctor forbids him absolutely the sea air, for this year, on account of the irritated state of his lungs and bronchia.[1] So he hoped to be able to go and pay you a little visit and regrets very

[1] Before consulting the specialist Gissing had planned to spend the summer on the coast of Normandy.

much to have to give it up, at least for the present. We were glad to hear all goes well with you both. It was a great pleasure for me to make your acquaintance; I hope it will not be too long before I see you again. Give my kindest regards to Mr Wells and believe me, dear Mrs Wells, sincerely yours

GABRIELLE GISSING

73

GISSING TO WELLS

26 *April* 1901 13 *Rue de Siam, Paris*

MY DEAR WELLS, It was by the mercy of heaven that you came to Paris just when you did. Since that week, I doubt whether there has passed one day when both of us could have enjoyed your visit. Influenza, chiefly—with the result that I have at last had to consult a leading doctor, and behold his orders.

He absolutely forbids the seaside, says it might do me serious harm.[1] For a year I have had bronchitis added to my chronic emphysema, and it must be got rid of. I am to go either to a well sheltered station in the high Alps, or, if that be not possible, to a dry and sunny place right in the country. For the next month, before leaving Paris, I am to be in the hands of a subordinate doctor, who will

[1] In the margin of this paragraph Gissing wrote: "moist spot, also, on right lung."

scarify the chest on the right side, and administer hypodermic injections of something or other. Happily no drugs are ordered, merely as much food as possible. For the present, work has to cease—though only, I hope, for a week or two.[1]

Well now, this casts me down. I had lived, positively lived, on the hope of seeing an English field, and walking in an English lane, this summer. You know—or perhaps you do not quite know—what those words mean to me. Now I must go to the centre of France (I don't think the Alps are possible) and vegetate amid things which serve only to remind me that here is *not* England. Then again, I had thought night and day of a boiled potato—of a slice of English meat—of tarts and puddings—of teacakes; night and day had I looked forward to ravening on those things. Well, well!

Don't write for the present; it will only distress me. But let Mrs Wells, if she will be so kind, and if it does not tire her, answer Gabrielle's letter. As you may imagine, Gabrielle is very good through all this. It was bad enough for her to pass her life as nurse to her mother; now she has me also to worry about.

The worst is that of course I say to myself: Now, *suppose*, instead of consulting a doctor, I had gone for three months to Sandgate; and *suppose* it had done me

[1] Despite the serious deterioration of his health during the preceding three months, Gissing had by this time written almost half of *Veranilda*.

enormous good?—I cannot regard the supposition as an impossibility; does a French doctor take into account the fact that Englishmen's native air is that of the sea? I might, in following instinct, have done the right thing; and, as it is, I may be about to lose the whole of a precious summer. But of course I can feel no certainty; having taken the doctor's opinion, and finding it so very emphatic, I must needs follow it.

I rejoice that you are well. You shall hear again before we leave Paris. Every good wish and thought to you both.

Yours always,
GEORGE GISSING

74

GISSING TO WELLS

21 *May* 1901 13 *Rue de Siam*, *Paris*

MY DEAR WELLS, The Editor of *Literature*[1] has asked me to sit to Elliot & Fry. As, in my circumstances, I dare not reject any decent advertisement that offers, I must come to London for two or three days, and hope to get no ill by it. Indeed, after a month's rest and open air, I am greatly better.

The date is not settled; it will probably be during the

[1] Frank Arthur Mumby (1872–1956). The portrait of Gissing appeared in *Literature* on 20 July 1901.

next 8 days. Now, I am asking myself whether your domestic circumstances will make it possible to give me a bed for a night, coming and going. If there is the least doubt, you will of course simply say that our meeting must be postponed, and in that case I should probably take a cheap Whitsuntide ticket via Newhaven. But it would do me good to see you, if it involves no difficulty.

I don't know whether I am incurring a risk for nothing —perhaps you will think the *Literature* portrait a matter of small importance. Let me have your opinion on a card, will you?

Kindest remembrances from Gabrielle to Mrs Wells.

Ever yours,
GEORGE GISSING

75

GISSING TO WELLS

24 *May* 1901 — 13 *Rue de Siam*, *Paris*

MY DEAR WELLS, Thanks for your letter, and old E's excellent portrait.

Now listen. Gabrielle has been headachey of late, and it would be *just* possible for her to get away from home for four days. May I bring her with me? Programme:

Monday (27) arrive at Sandgate and spend night.
Tuesday. Go on to London, and to Pinker's.

Wed. Pinker's.

Thurs. Back to Sandgate.

Friday. Back to Paris.

If there be the shadow of an objection, you will state it kindly but unmistakably.[1] If there be none, you will send a post-card (not a letter) posted early on *Saturday*, so that I may have it on Sunday here.

All good be with you both.

Yours,

G. G.

Henry James[2] and Conrad? If G. be with me? What think you? Is it advisable?

76

GISSING TO WELLS [postcard]

Friday [24 *May*]

I of course omitted from my letter the essential point, that I have at least 2 days' business in London, and on that account gladly accept Worcester Park[3] hospitality. The brave P. has been very kind with repeated invitations.

G. G.

[1] The Gissings did leave on May 27 as here planned.

[2] Wells and Gissing spent a night with Henry James at Rye. Gissing enjoyed James's Georgian house and his reminiscences of Turgenev.

[3] Pinker lived in Worcester Park.

77

GISSING TO MRS WELLS

26 May 1901 13 *Rue de Siam, Paris*

DEAR MRS WELLS, Your sunshine letters come on a morning of cloud and cold. Three weeks of hot sunshine; now,—of course—sudden change to winter. We can only hope that it will be *not* worse to-morrow. If it *should* be worse, I dare not face it, and should await the weather of Tuesday.[1] If Tuesday prove impossible, Gabrielle must give up the visit altogether, as she is bound to be back here, in any case, not later than Sunday, and the time would be too short. (On the 10th we hope to leave for Autun and of course there is endless trouble with regard to shutting up of the flat, etc.) But we shall assuredly come to-morrow (yes, by the boat arriving at 4) if the weather be not *very* bad, and, if driven to it, then on Tuesday.

Now let me speak of all your kind suggestions. Unfortunately it is not for E. & F. alone that I must go to London; I have other business. Nevertheless, if Way[2]

[1] In the margin Gissing wrote: "Noon. Weather greatly improved. Ho for tomorrow." He and Gabrielle did carry out their original plan, for on May 29 Pinker wrote to Wells, "Mr and Mrs G. arrived last night. How very ill he looks. She is charming."

[2] Hal Way, an old pupil of Wells and an employee of Elliot & Fry, was the photographer who took most of the portraits in the *Literature* series.

would come to Sandgate (say on Friday or Saturday) it would be pleasanter. But how am I to act? Is Way an independent volition? Can he be addressed directly? E. & F. write to me that they will arrange a desk for me to sit at, as the Editor of *Literature* insists on a *mise-en-scène*. Now, obviously I must not be taken with the background of the brave H. G's study! But perhaps you also could "arrange a desk" elsewhere than in the study.

(I interrupt myself to marvel at you both. How you can earn a living, and at the same time be absolutely at the disposal of every vagabond friend who chooses to invade you, I cannot even conjecture.)

Now for Worcester Park. The fact of the matter is that I very much wish to show this courtesy to Mrs Pinker. This morning I have a letter from herself, very kind indeed. Immediately after your return from Paris, Pinker wrote inviting us both whenever we should be in England. I feel that we *ought* to go to Worcester Park, and indeed it would be a pleasure to do so under the circumstances. The plan is to arrive there *for dinner* on Tuesday, and on *Thursday* morning to return to Sandgate.—Pinker is a good fellow, and I wish for an opportunity of showing him that I appreciate his human qualities.

Gabrielle (who for a week has had a sore throat) is busy packing. She wishes me to tell you that your letter has given her much joy, and that the prospect of next week delights her. I hope to goodness the weather will not turn winterly. Indeed, it will make me quite ill if I have to telegraph our inability to start. I hope better things.

Very sincerely yours,

GEORGE GISSING

78

GABRIELLE GISSING TO MRS WELLS

10 *June* [1901] *Paris*

DEAR MRS WELLS, I am quite sure everything you are doing [1] is meant for the good of my husband and I have to thank you and Mr Wells heartily for your extreme kindness to him and the most affectionate interest you take in him.—But necessarily our native differences do not allow me to appreciate everything as you do.—I am accustomed to the ways of French doctors, you to English. Of course no French doctor would ever dream of taking away an invalid from his wife—provided his wife is decent enough—to put him in the care of strangers. First of all he would think the fact would prove fatal simply on account of the invalid's feeling. Then French doctors attach a great importance to the solicitude of the

[1] Gabrielle accompanied Gissing on his visit to England in May but returned to France before his consultation with Dr Pye-Smith. Mrs Wells must have informed Gabrielle that Gissing was to remain in England for treatment. This reply shows the tensions created by Gabrielle's high-pitched temperament, her patriotism, the burden of her invalid mother, the fear of Gissing's legal wife, and jealousy of his family.

person who looks after the invalid, day after day, to the knowledge this person gets of the peculiarities of the invalid, of his illness, of the various and numerous little symptoms which develop and very often can even guide the doctor in his treatment of the case.—I know English doctors do not preoccupy themselves so much with such details.—But I can speak of this fact in full knowledge, unfortunately, as from the age of 14 I have had my mother an invalid, always with serious matters, at first the chest, then the heart, and she has never had another nurse than myself, so that, without having made special medical studies, I have got a too good knowledge of illnesses, treatments, nursing, etc., and I remember how often a doctor turned to me, asking for this or that small detail unobserved by a person who has no devoted interest in the invalid.

Do not believe I make these remarks in order to undermine the decision you announce me, and be sure I did not breathe a word like that in any letter to George. I do not feel qualified to assume such a heavy, a grave responsibility, fighting against so many people, and probably the invalid himself. And certainly if he is now as strongly convinced that France would be his death, as he was, 3 years ago, that England would be, imagination being so powerful over the body, it would perhaps act quite in that way. Of course it would be a bitter trouble to me if I could admit for a moment the idea that his ruined health dated from the day when our married life began, only 2 years ago. Fortunately, I have a lot of letters he wrote to me, just before, from Dorking, giving me a detailed and terrible report of his state of health: the doctor finding a decided phthisis at the right lung, emphysema, eczema very troublesome, no appetite, beginning of losing weight, long quite sleepless nights spent in pacing his room with such shouting and shrieking that his housekeeper thought at first he was mad and was frightened. And all that, he said, was due to the frightful state of his nerves, after the frightful life he had lived. And he felt convinced the climate did him harm, and the solitude too, and the change and the happiness would give him health again. And it was with this hope and persuasion that I consented to become his wife without delay, though I had my mother, just a widow and very ill, whom I would have never accepted to leave alone, and though I foresaw on this account great difficulties and embarrassments. Of course I was very grateful to my mother who so kindly allowed me to follow my heart's impulse and the voice of my conscience, and to do a thing so much in contradiction to all her family traditions and her own feelings.

No, I am quiet on this point: I know perfectly well France has not been fatal to my husband. I remember too well last winter when his cough had quite disappeared and he did *not* get a *trace* of cold—which had not happened since 10 years at least, he said.—Now, you speak of managing to put my mother in good hands to be able to join my husband. The thing is not quite as easy as you imagine. You were fortunate enough to have your mother in perfect health; mine is quite at the end of her days; lately the doctor warned me that she could die suddenly at any moment, her heart and arteries being quite worn out. It is a miracle that she is still alive. Indeed I was much alarmed in leaving her, a fortnight ago, and was every day afraid of getting a fatal telegram. On my coming back I was startled with the change that had come on her features, and in the night after, I positively thought she was dead! You see in what painful position I find myself.

But that is not all—far from it.—Perhaps you are aware that George always regarded as a great danger, in fact as an impossible thing, our living in England, and even my being with him for long, settled in some place. It is more than ever dangerous: the woman to whom he is legally bound has begun, lately, to travel about in England, in pursuit of him, she has been to Wakefield and I have no doubt she will easily enough find out where he will live, seize him and give herself the pleasure—she has every right to do so—of restoring him to the brilliant state of health and nerves he enjoyed when in care of her. You will admit that I cannot accept the idea of a conflict with this lady, and of the scenes it would lead to, which would not be quite suitable for George's state, as far as I can judge.

Again: I think it very possible that his own family will like to come and have their holidays with him. And I can't help having a suspicion that he would be himself much more pleased to have his sisters' company than mine. I know what a power they have over him, what admiration he has for everything they think, say or do.—I cannot forget that last April, after I had done my utmost during a year to nurse him and protect him against every possibility of cold, he fled away like a madman to see them, in the most horrible weather, turning away from all my supplications and tears—because I knew only too well what would happen and of what we now bear the results!—he ran every risk possible of breaking down, and that without an hesitation. So that, I am afraid—and it is painful enough for me—that if choice had to be made, it would not be in my favour. Or, things have altered since last year—it may be so.—But, in any case, how am I to forbid his family—mother, sisters, child, to come to him when in England? And you know it would be impossible for me to meet them; they do not even know of my existence, George having never dared to hurt their feelings and incur their remonstrances on this point. For them, I should be an object of unspeakable contempt, and *that* I shall never be able to bear.—I cannot bear humiliations like that, I am too proud.—I have certainly made great sacrifices, of half the natural joys of every married woman, but I cannot bring myself to be treated with scorn and contempt, assimilated to a low and vulgar creature. That is quite impossible for me.

You see, dear Mrs Wells, how things really are!—Of course if George expressed a desire of seeing me, and if he were getting worse, if he were in imminent danger of death, I should fly without a thought and try to see him, if possible, just for a moment. Ah! I could write this letter to you with tears better than with ink!—Such complete misery and distress is impossible to express! I feel that, from the moment I left him on the deck, a week ago, everything is finished for me. What can I be for him now? What can I do? Nothing. Nothing. Helplessness and desolation. That is all that remains to me.—

Please tell me: have I to understand that he is in actual danger? That he is threatened by what we call in French a "*phtisie galopante*"? (That means which takes you away in a very short time, a few months.) I should like to know whether he still coughs, as he did whilst I was with you?—because when he did the "*cacodylate de soude*" treatment and the burning points he nearly entirely ceased to cough—and he had coughed ceaselessly since May of last year.—

I beg you to excuse my bad English and this very long letter, dear Mrs Wells. I wished to thank you before, you and Mr Wells, for the kind and charming hospitality you have given me. My kindest regards to all of you. Believe me very affectionately yours

GABRIELLE

Kindly give my love to George.

79

GABRIELLE GISSING TO WELLS

Châlet Feuillebois, Coulsard,
24 *June* [1901] *près Autun, Saône et Loire*

My dear Mr Wells, I thank you for your very friendly letter which I should have already answered, had I not been rather ill and quite incapable of writing and thinking.—I assure you I perfectly know and appreciate the great liberality of the best English people on the point which concerns me—it would indeed be very unkind of me if I did not—and I should quite agree with all you say, I think just as you do about the Wakefield and legal Mrs G. questions, if George was a man of the same nature and disposition as you, if he were able to feel or *act* as you would. In that case, yes, these dreads and fears I expressed would be very stupid and unjustified, but *as it is* I know only too well they are *not*. You can believe I know G. very well, perhaps better than anybody else can, after having lived with him for two years, day by day, through many circumstances and great or small details of every day life which bring out fully the most intimate part of one's nature. I think I know him in every corner of his caracter and can't deceive myself now. If I seem to you absurdly timid it is because I know how impossible it is to feel absolutely sure and safe with him, on account of what you call his "cowardice," with something else added to it: an extraordinary, terrible, perhaps morbid *unstability* in mind, views, decision, feelings (I at least mean in the things of ordinary life), a quite peculiar unability of being happy for a long time in unchanged circumstances, and surroundings. That, you can't fully realize, I think, without constantly living with him for a year or two.—I had, however, detected and feared it already before becoming his wife, but I had tried to persuade myself that this dangerous disposition was one of the bad results of the peculiarly sad and miserable life he told me he had had all along and that it could be cured like everything else by what we both thought would be happiness for him. Now I have come to know that it is a constitutional feature of his quite in his blood, like his physical disease, and unfortunately uncurable—that.

I have come to think, in trying to explain to myself that strange, rather abnormal unstability of caracter, constant changing of moods (I know it is very frequent in artists, but not in that degree), I have come to think that his health itself requires a great deal of changing; a change and for some time he feels better and happy, then the bad germ in him, the uncertainty of his health reappears, he feels the want of another change and gets discontented, hating his present conditions of living—and so on and so on.

Of course that makes life very difficult and a sudden decision very grave to take. With a man of moods like that you have to try constantly to adapt every material or moral circumstance to his actual, temporary mood. And if you had him only to think about! But no, there are other people you have to coexist with, who have an immense part in his life and thoughts and feelings.

My dear Mr Wells, I assure you I don't exaggerate a bit the influence and preponderancy of Wakefield over him—perhaps he is not even conscious of it—. But you say yourself that you know how terribly Wakefield weighs upon him. And how true that is! That simple fact of his not daring to tell them the truth about his marriage with me, saying he had "to spare their feelings."[1] Do you think I was not *deeply hurt* by that,—though I said nothing? And once, quite in the beginning, when he said to me he knew he was quite right in doing what he did in marrying me, "because he had to live *for his children*"?—And some unhappy words like that, which I succeeded in removing from my mind, but which come back again in the hours of solitude and misery. I know he would not have said them now—or I think so,—and yet! . . .

Do you know I was doomed to be apart from him this summer. Not long before our going to England he had decided to go from Autun straight to north England in August and spend a month or two with his people there—of course without me. And as I, knowing he was ill, expressed my anxiety at such a project because supposing

[1] See Letter 38, note 2.

by some accident if he happened to be very ill there, and I being not permitted to go and join him, what torture should I live in, what should I do? He replied: "You would get news through Miss Collet or the Wellses." Now what do you think of that? Would you have ever said that to Mrs Wells? And is it not the best proof of the extraordinary dependance he has towards the Wakefield people?

And you must not imagine that I don't believe he loves me and cares for me. I should be cruelly wrong and unjust if I did not. Certainly, I must confess I have had doubts about that and rather difficult and painful moments in the first year of our married life (*nobody* in the world except you now knows that) and I should have very much preferred to have all these people living *with* us, *beside* us, rather than *between* us, as I have so often felt. But during the last year, little by little, our intimacy has grown, and more confidence has come about and we had come to understand each other so well—which is certainly not a proof of bad domestic circumstances—that I can't be mistaken about his feelings towards me more than I am about mine towards him. I love him and I would not dream of complaining about his circumstances—which I knew from the first as well as he knew mine—but I had not, I *could* not, imagine from what he told me, this extraordinary intimacy and domination of Wakefield with him. And of that I am sure he is partly unconscious; it is stronger than him, than his will; the voice of the blood, these old habits overcome him from time to time; in fact they rule him.

I had recently a new example of that. His sisters suddenly wrote telling they could no longer endure his boy, he was getting so arrogant, selfish, undisciplined, etc.; he would have to go to a larger school and they named one of very high terms.[1] Poor G., already ill and unable to work, was in despair, and so upset that he could not help speaking to me about the matter. We had a few dreadful days and nights on account of that, but it had been decided he had to ask the advice of Miss Collet (perhaps you know her), who is very strong and intelligent on all these subjects. And indeed she replied, plainly disapproving of the sister's proposed school on precisely the same reason I had pointed out to G.—Moreover she had taken informations and strongly recommended a school of whose master she personally knows and thinks highly.

Poor George was delighted and resolute. But he wrote to Wakefield and then came furious letters and a battle was engaged against Miss Collet (whom they dis-

[1] Walter had been in the Wakefield Boys' Preparatory School where Ellen Gissing was a member of the staff. I have been unable to identify the schools referred to in the passage that follows, but from Ellen's letter of 21 May 1904 to Wells it is clear that Walter was then attending Gresham's School, Holt, Norfolk at a cost of £42 a year. It is also clear the Ellen was enthusiastic about the school and its effect on Walter. According to Miss Orme's letter of 27 May 1904 to Wells, the younger son Alfred was living with a farming family at a yearly charge of £19.

like), and her proposal, telling the school she advised was not an aristocratic sphere, etc., and urging George in the same tone they would have used with a helpless irresolute boy to leave this business entirely in their hands (the money part excepted, of course) as they were so vastly superior in all these questions, and to give Miss C. never mind what pretext for not following her advice. And they indeed did not wait for their brother's reply and consent and quite without his knowing sent the child away to a school after their own ideas. And when G. discovered that, by chance,—when we were with you, he was quite pleased and admirative about the decision and ability of his sisters.

Well, that is an example between a thousand. And certainly, knowing all that and much more so subtle that can't be expressed do you wonder if I really doubt, suppose his sisters put him in the alternative of choosing between them and his child—and me, whether even loving me, he would not feel easier to decide in their favour. I hope I am quite wrong and I should be terribly distressed if he could suspect these vague fears of mine, (I can add that *I think* secretly that *I am* wrong), but you would no doubt understand this strange, confused, instinctive dread of Wakefield if you had seen and especially *felt* so many little things, little troubling things, desolating for a wife who can't bear to feel someone *between* her and her husband. Beside, yes; but *between*, and secretly between, what is worse, that is very hard.

Do you know you would perhaps have never heard of his union with me if *I* had not urged him again and again to let you know the truth and not keep me in such mystery, apart from all his family and friends. And my recent stay with him at your house which I enjoyed so much was due to the fact of my mother telling G.: "But why don't you take Gabrielle with you? It would do her good." Then he welcomed the suggestion, but I am sure he was a little afraid of doing so rash a thing!

And when you speak of the legal *Mrs* G. you have no idea of the terrorising power she has on him. Were it not that, he could never have come to such extreme misery with her. You speak of his stopping her allowance, but don't you know that this allowance was *raised* just before our marriage, on the first grumbling and complaint and threatening of this creature?[1] (I must say I think G. has a very silly solicitor.) And, by the by, if you really think such thing is possible, it seems to me it would be the right moment of—if not absolutely stopping—at least lowering this allowance on the account of G's state, disease, with necessity of long treatment, unability to work, by absolute constatation of the doctor, and so on.

You say that woman would not possibly find us out in England, but how did she discover G's abode when he was at Dorking and so carefully concealed his address, and how is it that she came down straight to the place and asked for him and was admitted, and he gave her tea,

[1] Edith asked for £2 a week.

and so on,—at a moment we were already engaged together?—No, I think it is a real kindness to George to spare him possible, not to say probable, troubles of that sort, which he has not the nervous strength necessary to face, to bear, to overcome.

Now, my dear Mr Wells, if I don't worry you too much with this endless letter, let me tell you that my deep desire would be of course to go and join my husband to shorten our sad, deplorable separation—on more than one account—If I don't do that now it is wrong to attribute it simply to my attachment to other duties. Putting aside the very uncertain state of my health just now which requires care there are other reasons which prevent me from going. First of all, where could I possibly go? I don't think doctors admit gladly ordinary people amid their invalids at the sanatorium, and to go and live simply in the neighbourhood would not be very satisfactory. Then there is a very silly, sordid and despisible question—but unfortunately not neglectable—the money question. You are perhaps not aware of that question being the constant worry and chief anxiety of G's daily life. He has very heavy burdens: the woman, children, mother and sisters—even brother,[1] if you had

[1] Algernon Gissing, a writer of local-colour novels, was constantly in need of money. To relieve George from anxiety in this matter Ellen wrote confidentially to Wells in June 1902, asking him to find a post for Algernon which would provide an income but which would not check his writing. Wells turned to Gosse, who secured £100 from the Royal Literary Fund.

seen him, as I did, constantly gloomy and miserably brooding over his pecuniary situation, anguish troubling him all day long, preventing him of sleep; his nervous trembling state at every bill I showed him—though reduced to the minimum possible by the most incredible care in every detail—you would understand that I consider as a duty towards him to spend the summer where I am, the rent being already paid and the living cheap. I know he will have large expenses to do for his health, and that he ought not to work for a rather long time and that he would not benefit in his health as soon as the troubles about money begin again.

Of course I don't enjoy without him my stay here (in the place he had himself desired and chosen after his own taste, quite solitary in the country) though the country is very hilly and magnificent, and the air beautiful and weather splendid. All these things sadden me rather. But these are small considerations, and I *know* too well what I have in mind is of first importance for him.

I must end—at last! Let me tell you that, remembering all last year, our peaceful life, our quiet talks in the evenings, both together, our intimacy and union steadily growing, I am simply amazed at the strange complaining which has suddenly begun, and is going on from him. I should not be far from thinking his brain as ill as his lungs if I knew him less. Discontent is in his nature, I repeat it; paradise is always for him where he is not—I mean settled. Believe me, it would be a most dangerous and bad business to encourage him in his discontented moods. With regard to practical life, everyday life, George is like a child. Nobody—even the most fortunate—can avoid many little worries which a day brings and another takes away, but as soon as George comes in contact—immediate or intermediate—with one, he thinks it is due to his actual circumstances, a part of them, a thing that would never happen if these circumstances altered. That is the constant delusion of his mind, a product of his bad health and his deep unpracticality.

Excuse me, my dear Mr Wells, I pray, and believe I am very unhappy indeed just now! I beg Mrs Wells to accept here my kindest regards and best wishes.

Sincerely yours

GABRIELLE GISSING

Of course I beg you to destroy this confidential letter, which, I hope you will consider as the best proof of my regarding you both as my best friends, as well as of George.[1]

Will you be able to understand my English?

[1] In *Experiment in Autobiography*, VIII, 3, Wells referred to Gabrielle's letters and recalled that after one or two vain attempts to bring about a better understanding between Gabrielle and Gissing, he "brutalized the situation" and announced that he would not "read through, much less paraphrase, consider or answer any further letters" from her. This may explain the fact that Gabrielle addressed her next letter to Mrs Wells.

80

GISSING TO MRS WELLS

East Anglian Sanatorium, Nayland, Suffolk[1]

25 *June* 1901

DEAR MRS WELLS, The place is beautiful, and the system, evidently, all it claims to be; but—it isn't like living at Spade House. I am only just beginning to feel the loneliness; things will be dark enough in a week's time. But here are men and women in obvious process of cure, and I must bear it for a while. Among the patients confined to the bedroom is a man called Garrett,[2] whom it was thought likely I should know—a man recently back from S. Africa. Do you know anyone of that name?

Well, to begin with I was sternly sent to bed, and kept there for a day and a half—above me a poor woman who coughs day and night, and tears my heart with pity. I am just up again, but condemned to absolute idleness. The feeding is stupendous. I thought of you when, just

[1] Although Dr Hick did not believe that Gissing had tuberculosis, he advised a consultation with Dr Pye-Smith who strongly recommended the "open air and over-feeding cure" at Dr Jane Walker's newly opened sanatorium in Suffolk.

[2] Fydell Edmund Garrett (1865–1907) was appointed editor of the *Cape Times* in 1895 and was influential in African affairs until broken health compelled him to return to England in 1899. After his graduation from Cambridge he had served on the staff of the *Pall Mall Gazette* to which Wells was a regular contributor.

now at dinner, a person next me refused strawberries, and the girl waiting exclaimed sharply—"O but you must!"

I hear of strange cures. A parson came here to die; scarce a hope for him. In 14 months he was sent away a sound man.

A young woman with whom I have talked at table seems to be deeply dyed with literary associations—is going to be visited by the Editor of the *Quarterly*.[1] She spoke to-day of H. G. W., you, and was loud in praise of *The Wheels of Chance* and *Love and Mr Lewisham*, intelligent praise, moreover. It is rare to find anyone who prefers those two, and knows why.

I have a line from Gabrielle, just to say that she is safe at Autun. The distance is a misery; I didn't feel it so much at Sandgate. It is difficult to believe that I shall ever see her again.

Hick goes on well, I hope. Amid his illness, he dictated a long letter about me to Dr Walker. Good creature!

I meant to say something about those weeks at Spade House,[2] but I had better not. I live only for one hope,

[1] George Walter Prothero (1848–1922).

[2] According to Morley Roberts, Gissing's emaciation so disturbed Mrs Wells that she "fed him for all that she was worth." Gissing gained seven pounds within the first week. Dr Hick had planned to have Gissing stay in his home but was able to accommodate him for only a few days. (*The Private Life of Henry Maitland*, pp. 197 ff. and *Experiment in Autobiography*, VIII, 3.)

that you and the Anticipator[1] may some day sit with Gabrielle and me at our own table under our English roof. That will never be, most likely, but it would be an honest joy.

Meanwhile, all good be with you both.

Yours ever,

George Gissing

81

GISSING TO WELLS

25 *June* 1901 *East Anglian Sanatorium, Nayland*

My dear Wells, Many thanks for the *Westminster Gazette*.[2] The books are getting their chance, at all events.

All goes well here. I cough very little, and put on weight slowly—it is evident that I cannot add very much more without inconveniences. The scoundrel psoriasis yields slowly.

Dr Walker makes a good impression. She has been invited, I hear, to read a paper at the forthcoming inter-

[1] This is a play upon Mrs Wells's pregnancy and Wells's *Anticipations of the Reaction of Mechanical and Scientific Progress upon Human Life and Thought*, then being serialised in the *Fortnightly Review*.

[2] The *Westminster Gazette* (27 June 1901) praised *By the Ionian Sea* at some length and in the highest terms. The reviewer took special notice of Gissing's choice of a little-travelled region of Italy and emphasised, unduly, his interest in antiquity.

national congress on Tuberculosis—a distinction which must mean something. Her view of my case is cheerful enough; she seems to think that a few weeks will see me as well as I can ever expect to be.

You are working quietly and reasonably, I hope—would to heaven I had your cause for peace of mind! But some day, perhaps.

The most interesting person here is a Miss White,[1] a classical tutor at Newnham—a very vigorous type, who will serve me one of these days. Humorous, erudite, smokes cigarettes—the friend of everybody one can mention. On the whole, there is a pleasant gathering; nobody offensive.

Will you kindly address the enclosed and post as soon as possible?

Letters between here and Autun take 4 days and more. It is ill work corresponding in such conditions. Of course I shall act on your suggestion, and go out there as soon as possible; I dare not (indeed cannot) do otherwise. As always in things practical, I bungled this affair from the first. Whether it means the end of all the best things I had hoped has still to be seen.

Very kind remembrances to Mrs Wells—nay, in plain truth, hearty love to both of you.

George Gissing

[1] Rachel Evelyn White (1867–1943) was Lecturer in Classics at Newnham College, Cambridge, from 1899 to 1926.

82

GABRIELLE GISSING TO MRS WELLS

12 *July* [1901] *Châlet Feuillebois, Coulsard*

MY DEAR CATHERINE, I awaited every day the great news of you,[1] but as it may delay a little, perhaps, I will not wait longer to thank you heartily for all your and Mr Wells's kindness to George and the good his stay with you has done him. I am glad to hear he continues to improve, though not at the same rate, I think, as in the beginnings, at yours. He wrote it was very hot lately. I do not think you feel much the heat at the seaside, and we don't here too, on account of the situation high up above a vast plain and amid wooded mountains from which comes a delicious cool breeze, good and enjoyable amid hot continually glaring sunshine.

What we shall do next winter, I don't know and it is not very easy to decide—George wishes to settle down somewhere in the country quickly, but I don't think taking a hasty step a very wise thing, as I have not his inclination for change and am not willing to move every year or so (as it has been his custom all his life). Moreover it would be well to have a doctor's advice about the place to choose, and to go about, see and compare before deciding. Well, we shall see.

[1] See Letter 83.

Now, about the question spoken of in Mr Wells's kind last letter (of course *you* have read it, and I always intend my letters, however addressed to you or him, being for both of you), I shall certainly do my best to please George in everything, but I entreat you not to think his strange complaints about not being master in his household and just mistress etc., quite justified. Good George has the faculty of getting strange fancies in his head and to be easily wrong in things of that kind. He has no idea whatever about the realities of domestic life, but thinks he has, and as his criterion in that as in every thing is Wakefield, if something is different, it is immediately condemned. Do you remember his exclamation at your speaking of camphoring the winter things for summer? Well, I could see that was one of his complaints in my domestic arrangements, as well as mending of socks and so on, because they never do things like that at Wakefield; "that spares time," he says admiringly. All his complaints resemble this, more or less. You will understand it, I think.

You know in a house where there is only one servant and you wish everything to be in order and well done, and not overtax your servant, you are obliged to occupy yourself a good deal with all that (especially when it is obligatory that everything should be managed with the greatest economy possible). Our servant is a very honest girl, in every respect, and cooks well, but she has no memory whatever and you have to repeat her twenty times a thing and even to see her doing it, if you will be sure of its being done. Servants question has become a very difficult one on the continent and you can't turn out of your house a good girl simply on that account, at least you hesitate. Well, my mother (not from the first, true, but since a year, I repeat things have been bad in the first year; I was entirely discouraged, disheartened), my mother has in our household simply what I should call the *executive power*. She can't occupy herself, she can do nothing, and so she was willing to spare me these little worries of being preoccupied with what the servant would forget, etc., and my orders being given in the morning, see that they would be punctually executed. So that I had much more time to give to reading, and to my translations, my prime occupation of latest years. And I could too more easily go and see a friend, and so on. Of course George dislikes my going to see friends and would like me living in his own solitary way; but that I can't endure very long and I don't think it is a good thing, even for him. I only see people I really like and who interest me, but it is a great pleasure to me to see them and talk with—a very tranquil and honest pleasure, I think.

Of course in little apartments it is not easy at certain moments to conceal from everybody what is going on, so that if good George happens to see my mother speaking to the servant he immediately gets the idea (wrong) it is *she* who rules the household, dictates laws in the kitchen, etc. I in vain explain to him again and again the management; he does not believe me, *will* not. He is too glad to have found out a shadow to embody his latent—always latent—complaints, disquietude, discontent. You may be sure that as long as he has not found any, he dreadfully suffers from want of giving an appearance of consistency to that tormenting unquietness of his soul. He *can't* be unreservedly happy; it is not in his nature; and that is what makes it really hard to sacrifice without good reason someone to him: because you know it will be a useless sacrifice. After having complained about my not being alone to superintend domestic affairs, he will complain about my being to much absorbed by them, as he has already done a little (instance: camphoring.)—and if I quite abandon the servant to herself, he will find fault with the forgetting of things and the more careless spending of money. He, who looks frightened and thinks life is incredibly expensive in France when the account exceeds 200 francs a month.

Because that is another of his strangenesses; sums of money required from him by Wakefield or even the woman, always seem to him small and trivial indeed, but the expenses made in our household always seem extravagant, however modest and carefully managed. I hope good innocent George is prepared to manage so as to be able not to tremble at every monthly account in future, because he can't expect to get everything requested for his diet and to keep expenses so low!—I beg your pardon for troubling you with all these "*low*" details, but I think it better you should know things exactly.

Now the capital part of my letter, if you allow me, because I am greatly troubled about that new thing and I have a hope you both could help me in that. Do you know G., after his 6 weeks spent in the sanatorium, intends not to come quickly to me—as I always thought he would—but to rush to Wakefield and spend a week or ten days, he now says, but Heaven knows what it will be when he is there![1] In reading this project I thought I was dreaming! A man who, a month ago, writes me that Pye-Smith thought the journey back to Paris would cause his death, who has been so much advised not to fatigue himself, and who now would leave a sanatorium, a chosen air, and special careful conditions of life to rush in this extreme heat, wet with perspiration, to a smoky town like that, where he has already got his bad cold last year which brought him to his present state, and was not nursed at all, and making all this long, tiring journey, of course it is simply running the risk of loosing quickly all the good acquired in these two months and a half, of taking harm, falling ill and then being quite unable to travel again and to come and join me. Or to come to be ill on his arrival, just like last year.

I wrote to him, showing him as well as I could all that and imploring him to be more wise and prudent and to sacrifice that rash project to me, who have already had so

[1] See Letter 84, note 1.

sad a time and so long without him, adding that I would gladly do any sacrifice *for* his health but not for what I considered as being *against* it.—He simply replied he would do the thing prudently, if I thought Wakefield would be bad, he would invite all his people to meet him somewhere in a lodging, hotel, I don't know what. But that does not seem to me more prudent, as he will certainly require great care just on leaving that sanatorium, and follow a kind of treatment, etc., and choose the place he will be in. And how will he choose that place of meeting, and what a place to be in, a lodging or hotel, for an invalid, after a sanatorium!

I am most anxious about all that! And troubled by the fear of having our meeting indefinitely postponed, either by a relapse in his health occasioned by all that fatigue, rushing, heat, change of life, etc., or by the urging of his family. It is certain they will do their utmost to keep him with them and away from me as long as possible. And really it seems to me at the 6th or 8th of August, it will be high time we should be together again. Of course I quite understand his wish to see his boy and people and in another year and circumstances I should quite approve of his going to see them and spend some time with them; but *this* year, I think, is exceptional, and so much sacrifice has been required from me on account of his health that I think it right that everybody who loves him and he, himself, would do so now for the same reason. I think his people ought to *know* exactly the seriousness of his state; that perhaps would be good at many points of view. Could not Dr Hick let them know? And could not he and Mr Wells advise him not to do imprudent things which could ruin the possibility of his coming back to me? I feel sure you will feel as I do in that matter, or at all events understand my feeling and anxiety.

Of course I extremely dread the results of this stay and increased intimacy between him and his people, just before his intended returning to me, knowing as I only too well know his extreme, astonishing submissiveness to them. That will lead to troubles, I am afraid. And I know their love of exercising their authority over him, and their natural animosity against everyone who appears to have some influence on him! That is most dangerous, I think, just in this moment. Don't you and Mr Wells think so?

G. wrote to me that he had decided, *having heard your* opinion on the matter, to tell them the truth about us. Of course I replied how much I approved of that decision which I should have asked of him myself. In his last letter, about that beautiful project of Wakefield, he says he feels the more obliged to go and see them "*after what he is just going to tell them!*" (Underlined!) You can feel the shiver of terror going through him, can't you? Poor weak G.! And notice that he is convinced he has to tell them simply a *monstrosity*—feeling that is rather insulting for me, it seems.

But I must not worry you longer! I beg you again to excuse me. It is a very painful friend you have got in me, for the present. But things will change some day, I hope. I trust you are very well and happy in waiting for your baby. Will you be kind enough to let me know? I do wish you the best things and success. Remember me very kindly to Mr Wells and Mrs Robbins and believe me, dear Catherine, your affectionate friend

GABRIELLE GISSING

Do beg Mr Wells from me to accept gallantly this new torture of reading and understanding this English of mine! I am ashamed when I think of it! But I suppose it would tire you more to read handwritten French at such length.

I was extremely pleased to hear G.'s books were so well received and reviewed. I should like so much to know Mr Wells's and your opinion about *The Charlatan*?—Just before leaving Paris I met Izoulet and had a long talk with him about this book and his.[1] He asked me whether George had thought there was something in the theory of his *Cité Moderne* likely to be particularly pleasant and useful for what we call an "*arriviste*," such as Lashmar. He very much wishes to read the book and to become acquainted with G. himself.

[1] *La Cité Moderne: Métaphysique de la Sociologie* (1894) by Jean Izoulet (1854–1929) provided Lashmar the charlatan with his "bio-sociological" theory. In the prefatory note to *Our Friend the Charlatan* Gissing disavowed any satirical intention with respect to Izoulet's book, but he began the preface with the phrase, *Suum cuique*.

Mr Franck Brentano,[1] the philosopher, showed me a demonstration invented by an Austrian philosopher of a 4th dimension of space. Do you know it? Of course I did not understand at all, but I remember the material part of the thing.

83

GISSING TO WELLS

19 *July* 1901 *East Anglian Sanatorium, Nayland*

MY DEAR H. G., I am very glad indeed to hear that all is well over.[2] I know not whether you wished boy or girl, but probably Mrs Wells is satisfied. Every kind thing to her from me as soon as she can receive messages.

Do not write again yourself just yet, but ask Hick to let me know that all goes well.

Yours ever,

GEORGE GISSING

[1] Franz Brentano (1838–1917), the German philosopher and psychologist, played a part in the development of the Gestalt theory and the phenomenology of Edmund Husserl.

[2] George Philip Wells was born on 17 July 1901.

84

GISSING TO WELLS

2 *August* 1901[1] *Sanatorium, Nayland, Suffolk*

MY DEAR WELLS, I was very glad to have a card with good news from Hick. There is now, I hope, nothing to inquire about—troubles must be practically over. It will make a great change in your life, and doubtless for good.

The August *Anticipations* please me much.[2] I find a great deal that I can thoroughly agree with. This will make an altogether remarkable volume.

Of myself I can only say that I have got up to 10 stone 9, without clothing—which I think I ought not to go beyond. Cough practically gone, but emphysema worse than ever.

I shall hope to have news of the boy before long. Wish I could hope to see him come to years of conversation. May life go well with him.

Love to both of you,

GEORGE GISSING

[1] According to a letter of July 6 Gissing planned to leave the sanatorium on July 26, spend a week with his family in Yorkshire, and then return to France. (*Letters of George Gissing to His Family*, p. 377.)

[2] This instalment of *Anticipations* was entitled "The Passing of Democracy." In it Wells argued that the kind of democracy based on the elective party system would inevitably lead to Caesarism and war unless, as he hoped, a guild of social engineers emerged from the middle classes.

85

GISSING TO WELLS

21 *August* 1901 *Châlet Feuillebois, Conard, Autun*

MY DEAR WELLS, Mrs Wells's snapshot of Gabrielle laughing (you remember) has had great success. I hope the negative has not been destroyed; some day I should like to ask for another copy.

We talk of you day by day, and hope all goes well. What, bythebye, is the name of the infant? Let us know.

This place is delightful; from our garden, a view over the picturesque old town, with a far horizon of great hills beyond. Out of Italy, I know no town so mediaevally attractive. It consists largely of seminaries and convents; the only noise is the ringing of bells.

The air, very fine. We are at a height of 1200 feet, and always have a breeze. That I am not likely to lose here what I gained at Nayland is clear from the fact that last week I gained little more than 1 kilo in weight.[1]

I am working for about a couple of hours each morning on *An Author at Grass*.[2] Rather miserable, to be

[1] In his diary Gissing later expressed a different opinion: "Place very damp and did me much harm." (*Letters of George Gissing to His Family*, p. 376.)

[2] This was the first title of *The Private Papers of Henry Ryecroft*, which Gissing began to write on 1 September 1900, two days after he finished *Our Friend the Charlatan*. He completed it within two months, and he was now revising and expanding it.

reduced to this stint, I who rejoiced in my good 8 hours per diem and always wrote better at the end than at the beginning.

Gabrielle sends her love to Mrs Wells, with all good wishes and hopes for the new inhabitant of Spade House. If you see H. H., please tell him I flourish. And remember me, I beg, occasion befalling, to Henry James and to Conrad.

Dr Walker (Jane) liked best of your books *The Wonderful Visit.*[1] So, I find, do many people. Not I, though, as you know.

This is Burgundy. Think of living in Burgundy, and not daring to drink wine! An experiment led to exasperation of emphysema.

Sandgate is at its sunniest just now, no doubt. Recall me to the Pophams. I do not ask to be remembered to Mrs Croker.[2]

All good be with you

Ever yours,

GEORGE GISSING

[1] In *The Wonderful Visit*, published in September 1895, a vicar brings down a bird which proves to be an angel. He shelters the wounded visitor, with interesting results among the neighbours.

[2] Mrs B. M. Croker (d. 1920), an acquaintance of Mrs Wells, wrote many popular novels.

86

GISSING TO MRS WELLS

c/o Mademoiselle Saglio, Fourchambault, Nièvre
10 *November* [1901]

Dear Mrs Wells, We ought to have written to tell you that we had left Autun, and are staying with friends at a place not very far from there—a country house overlooking the Loire. At the present moment, Gabrielle and I are in Paris, where we have come for a couple of days to get our winter clothing, for it is probable that we shall stay at Fourchambault until the end of the year. We are very glad to hear good news of you—of all three. Naturally, our state is not quite so cheery, but I have kept tolerably well through the vile weather of the last month or two, and have even gained considerably in weight—something like 10 lbs since coming to France. I manage to work a little, and hope to go on steadily through the winter.

An odd job I have on hand is an abridgment of Forster's *Life of Dickens* for Chapman & Hall[1]—which

[1] Chapman & Hall invited Gissing to prepare a new biography of Dickens by thoroughly revising Forster's *Life*. When Gissing asked £500 for the task the publishers offered £150 for an abridgement. Although Gissing cut up and reassembled two copies of the three-volume Forster, his work was more than a scissors-and-paste affair. A comparison of Forster's first chapter with the

I have undertaken to do in the next six months. I don't quite approve of this cutting down of good solid books—but £150 is offered for the work, which ought not to be very serious, and cash must be got one way or another. There is hope, I believe, of getting *An Author at Grass* decently published.

All about you are well I hope. Remember me, please, to Hick, if you see him. I picture the Pophams assailed by roaring tides. Let us, by all means, have a photograph of the young G. P.—Gabrielle wishes to be very kindly remembered to you both. To H. G. my affectionate greetings.

Always yours sincerely,
GEORGE GISSING

87

GISSING TO WELLS

21 *November* 1901 *Fourchambault, Nièvre, France*

MY DEAR OLD H. G., Your *Anticipations* was very welcome; no less so the second book which arrived this morning. Gabrielle is greatly pleased; by good chance,

---

redaction shows that Gissing changed almost a third of the sentences he retained. Although some of the alterations are no more than the insertion of a title or date, the difference is more substantial than is generally assumed. Gissing reduced the book to less than a quarter of its original length.

this happens to be her birthday, and no present could have been more acceptable. Hearty thanks, then, for both volumes.[1]

I have read *Anticipations*, and it seems to me that you have here done a very notable bit of work.[2] I must not pretend to care very much about the future of the human race; come what may, folly and misery are sure to be the prevalent features of life; but your ingenuity in speculation, the breadth of your views, and the vigour of your writing, make this book vastly enjoyable. The critical part of it satisfies and often delights me; you have told truths that clamour for the telling, and that in language quite your own. Stupidity should have a sore back for some time to come, and many a windbag (as Thomas used to say) will be uneasily aware of collapse. Those foot-notes, with their piquant familiarity, make one chuckle as well as think. And there are pages of rare charm, where a certain pathos touches the strain of satire—e.g. that describing the grey old general.[3]

[1] *Anticipations*, though dated 1902, was published in November 1901; *The First Men in the Moon* appeared in the same month after serialisation in the *Strand Magazine*.

[2] Writing to Arnold Bennett on 8 February 1902 Wells insisted that "something other"—and better—than story-writing and artistic merit had emerged in his recent books, especially in *Anticipations* but also in *The First Men in the Moon*, *The Invisible Man* and Chapter XXIII of *Love and Mr Lewisham*.

[3] In Chapter VI Wells satirically described an old general, splendidly uniformed and astride a horse, leading his column to doom in modern warfare.

Others are finely imaginative; the picture of "airy navies grappling in the central blue"[1] impresses one very strongly, and is one of your best bits of writing. For my own part, I have to confess that it made me sick and faint with horror—but none the less I felt its poetic beauty.

Are you serious in dating these things only a century from now?[2] I felt all along that verisimilitude required a lapse of at least five hundred years. But my opinion in such matters is worthless.

Bythebye, you speak of "God."[3] Well, I understand what you mean, but the word makes me stumble rather. I have grown to shrink utterly from the use of such terms, and, though I admit perforce a universal law, am so estranged by its unintelligibility that not even a desire to be reverent can make those old names in any way real to me.—This trifle apart, I much like your last chapter,

[1] Tennyson's "Locksley Hall," l. 124.

[2] In the 1924 preface to *Anticipations* Wells expressed obvious satisfaction in the accuracy of his forecasts: "Much of the guessing in it has been amply confirmed. . . . The tank appears in a footnote, sixteen years before it penetrated to the military intelligence of any country in the world."

[3] In the final chapter, to which Wells attached special value, he described God as the recognition of "an effect of purpose in the totality of things." He went on to say that the new men will "certainly not indulge in 'that something, not ourselves, that makes for righteousness' (not defined) or any defective clap trap of that sort." In a brilliant passage in *Ethical Studies* (1876) F. H. Bradley had denounced Arnold's phrase, "the Eternal not ourselves," as "nothing in the world but a piece of literary clap-trap."

and glad indeed am I to see the use of that word "home"[1] which you once (rightly enough no doubt) blamed me for dwelling upon too insistently in some story of my own.

Yes, it is a very notable book, and I hope even the dunderheads of the press will somehow give utterance to a truth or two about it. In any case, people who recognize power when they see it, will do you justice. You will have distinctly a stronger position after this—stronger because you have manifested to the multitude qualities which only the intelligent had noted and enjoyed.

Gabrielle tells me that we are going to Arcachon. I toil at my edition of "Forster,"[2] and feel pretty well. What are you doing? Love to all three of you.

Ever yours,

GEORGE GISSING

[1] In the final chapter Wells insisted that the "inevitable removal of births from the sphere of an uncontrollable Providence to the category of deliberate acts, will enormously enhance the responsibility of the parent." But Wells nowhere described *home* in terms more definite than the provision of "spacious opportunity" for a child.

[2] Gissing completed the abridgement of Forster toward the end of January 1902.

88

GABRIELLE GISSING TO WELLS

22 *November* [1901] *Fazières, Fourchambault*

DR MR WELLS, Thank you so much for having sent me this delightful book of yours. I only just glanced through it, enough to get quite eager to begin reading it. But, as I must now finish old *Tristram Shandy*, I will not delay my thanks to you until I am thoroughly acquainted with *The First Men in the Moon*. And, you already know with what interest George is reading *Anticipations*. He talks to me about it in a way to make me extremely anxious and impatient to read it too.

George is now weighing 77 kilos.—But, though his general state of health is very satisfactory, the state of his lung makes it advisable for him to spend the winter in the South-West, and he will soon depart for Arcachon where I shall accompany him. I hope all is well with you and your son is flourishing. We shall be glad to have his photograph. Please give my love to Mrs Wells to whom I will write soon, and believe me, dear Mr Wells, sincerely yours

GABRIELLE GISSING[1]

[1] The lack of further letters from Gabrielle is puzzling in view of the fact that Wells hastened to St Jean Pied de Port on 24 December 1903 when she telegraphed him that Gissing was dying.

89

GISSING TO MRS WELLS

30 *November* 1901 *Fourchambault*

DEAR MRS WELLS, I have never dared to subscribe to the press-cutters, for I remember too vividly the day when a press notice meant a sneer which disturbed my work. But, if ever you see anything which you think would interest me or please Gabrielle, you would do a kindness in sending it.

Next *Tuesday* (Dec. 3) we leave here.[1] Address will be:

Villa Souvenir
Arcachon
(Gironde)
France.

The name of the villa is an essential part of the address.

It rejoices me beyond measure to tell you that Courtney[2] seems disposed to print *An Author at Grass* in the

[1] Despite the statement in the preceding letter, Gissing was troubled by a persistent cough. Arcachon, situated on sandy hills which were covered by pine forests, provided protection against both dampness and wind. (*Letters of George Gissing to His Family*, pp. 379–380.)

[2] After some years in a post in philosophy at Oxford W. L. Courtney (1850–1928) entered journalism. As editor of the *Fortnightly Review* from 1894 until his death, he demonstrated a flair for subjects and writers.

Fortnightly. It is probably the best bit of work I shall do.

Pinker has not been yet to America, I think?

Love to you from Gabrielle, who is in good health and spirits. *The First Men in the Moon* has entertained us vastly. The astounding ingenuity of that husband of yours! Please pinch his ear for me.

Yours always, sincerely,

GEORGE GISSING

90

GISSING TO WELLS

22 *December* 1901 *Arcachon*

MY DEAR WELLS, With delight I see the quick editions of your book—may they hurry to the twentieth![1] This will add joviality to your Christmas. Of course we think and talk of you, and wish you all three every good thing.

Yours always,

GEORGE GISSING

Courtney takes *An Author at Grass*.[2]

[1] In a letter to Pinker (25 November 1901) Wells asked the meaning of "second edition" in the advertisments of *Anticipations*. Pinker replied, "The second edition means 3,000 in all, of which 750 are colonial." The third edition went to press on November 27.

[2] Gissing received £150 for the serial rights of *An Author at Grass*. Since the four parts of the book bore the names of the seasons, Courtney arranged the instalments as follows: "Spring" in May 1902; "Summer" in August; "Autumn" in November; and "Winter" in February 1903.

91

GISSING TO WELLS

19 *February* 1902 *Villa Souvenir, Arcachon, Gironde*

MY DEAR WELLS, Many thanks for your printed lecture.[1] The first feeling it moves in me is a keen regret that I could not have been present to hear you deliver it. I should have chuckled with contentment—for, oddly as it may sound, I have a real delight in the achievements and the success of those whom I personally like. You did well to accept that invitation. You are one of those who have something to say, and unless you get it said—said moreover, in a clearly effective way—there will be no rest for you.

This lecture is very good speaking—a vivid idea strongly and impressively worded. The bright strong hopefulness of the thing does one good. This optimism (as they call it) is your vigorous and effective side, and it well becomes you in the full healthy exercise of your life and your powers. Go on, and say all that you want to say; you can no longer be troubled by the fear that people do not heed you.

[1] Wells read a paper, "The Discovery of the Future," before the Royal Institution in January 1902. It appeared in *Nature* (6 February 1902) and was published as a book the same month.

Of course you are quite right about the *personal* unimportance of the "great" man.[1] He does not originate, but is merely fate's mouthpiece.

As eloquence, that is a fine passage in pp. 87–8.[2] But I am at some loss to grasp your meaning when you say that "there stirs something within us now that can never die again." Of course I put aside the vulgar interpretations of such words. Is it really, then, your conviction that the material doom of the Earth does not involve the doom of earthly life?—Anyhow, your declared belief in the "coherency and purpose" of things is pleasant to me. For I myself cannot doubt for one moment that purpose there *is*. On the other hand, I do doubt whether *we*—in

[1] In keeping with his argument that the twentieth century should free itself from the stranglehold of the past and creatively mould the conditions of the future, Wells was bound to depreciate the "Great Men" theory of history. Napoleon and Caesar, in his view, "were as much an outcome of systemic processes as are the pustules that break out through the skin of many growing young people." (*Experiment in Autobiography*, IX, 1.)

[2] The passage is as follows: "And finally, there is the reasonable certainty that this sun of ours must some day radiate itself towards extinction; that at least *must* happen; it will grow cooler and cooler, and its planets will rotate ever more sluggishly, until some day this earth of ours, tideless and slow moving, will be dead and frozen, and all that has lived upon it will be frozen out and done with. There surely man must end. That of all such nightmares is the most insistently convincing. And yet one doesn't believe it. At least I do not. And I do not believe in these things because I have come to believe in certain other things, in the coherency and purpose in the world and in the greatness of human destiny. Worlds may freeze and suns may perish, but I believe that there stirs something within us now that never can die again."

any sense of the pronoun—shall ever be granted an understanding of that purpose.

The weather here is cold and often very gloomy; I look anxiously for the first shimmer of spring. Let no man persuade you that the S.W. of France is "the south." The thermometer stands at zero (centigrade) day after day, and winds are often cutting.

I have lately made acquaintance with friends of Pinker's, Mr and Mrs Williamson,[1] who were here for a time. Pleasant people of the brightly prosperous and nomad order.—Bythebye, I suppose Pinker did *not* go to America, as he thought of doing?[2] But he has an office, I see, in New York.

How is Mrs Wells? How is G. P., the minim? I fear now and then that your breezes at Sandgate must be just a little *too* breezy. Does Hick flourish? A letter from him crossed one of them[3] at New Year's time, but I shall let

[1] In a letter to his sister Ellen, Gissing wrote, "On Christmas Eve, I found on my table a lot of splendid roses and white lilac and with them a visiting card on which was written 'From two admirers of the genius of Mr George Gissing.' . . . Of course I called on the Williamsons. They said they recognized me from my portrait. Well, well, and one can't make money enough to live quietly!" (*Letters of George Gissing to His Family*, p. 379.) Charles N. Williamson (1859–1920) was working on a series of articles on motoring in France. His American-born wife, Alice Muriel Williamson (1869–1933), recast these as letters, and the result was the popular book, *The Lightning Conductor* (1903). The numerous best-selling novels supposedly written in collaboration by the Williamsons were actually from the pen of Mrs Williamson.

[2] Pinker was in the United States in March–April 1902.

[3] ? A slip for "mine."

him hear again before long. I hope Popham bears the evil season well.

Gabrielle joins me in affectionate remembrances to you both.

Ever yours,
GEORGE GISSING

92

GISSING TO WELLS

26 *February* 1902 *Villa Souvenir, Arcachon*

MY DEAR WELLS, Many thanks for letting me see Gosse's letter, and thanks still more for the kindness which prompted you to send him my book.[1]

Bythebye, it seems to me that he quite misses the mark in what he says about your writing.[2] Right or wrong as

[1] Thanking Wells for a copy of *By the Ionian Sea*, Gosse wrote, "This is indeed a new phase of Gissing. It is as though a Salvator Rosa should suddenly produce a very delicate and perfect Watteau, all in pink and silver. I have always been a sincere admirer of Gissing, but this is quite a different thing, another Gissing evidently, and—I will not say better, but more to my personal taste."

[2] Wells had also sent a copy of *The Discovery of the Future* to Gosse, whose comment was, "I am sure the weak spot in all Utopias is the insufficient consideration of man's intense instinctive determination to be happy. You prophets of the future are so occupied with the useful that you forget that it is only in individualism that we can be happy." Gosse introduced this statement with the remark, "Our friend Gissing hits you shrewdly with his macello at Reggio"—an allusion to the description of a slaughterhouse in the last chapter of *By the Ionian Sea*.

to details, you certainly do not lose sight of the human demand for happiness—many people would say you took too much account of it.

Clodd has sent me an excellent little book of his on Huxley, just published.[1] You would like it, I think.

To-day, the Hugo Centenary, all schools in France give holiday, and there is something like a general fête all through the country. It is this kind of thing which makes one pardon so much in the French people. Morally, they are very low in the scale of nations—by morally, of course I mean all that the word implies; lower than I used to think. But this intellectual fervour is a good thing. When will England make holiday to celebrate any literary event?

Ever yours,
GEORGE GISSING

You see I have taken to the stylographic pen. It is rather offensive, as tending to obliterate character in handwriting;[2] but in the open air it gives one ease.

[1] In a letter of 1 March 1902 Gissing praised the book and thanked Clodd for several passages in it. (Clodd, *Memories*, pp. 179–182.)

[2] Gissing's handwriting, though regular, was so delicate and microscopic that publishers' advisers complained of the difficulty of reading his manuscripts.

93

GISSING TO WELLS [postcard]

28 *February* 1902 *Arcachon*

I have a letter from my old friend Bertz, in which he says: "Do you know that Wells's books are receiving great attention in Germany?"[1]—Unfortunately he gives no details.

Glorious spring weather!

G. G.

94

GISSING TO WELLS

Villa Lannes, Ciboure, St Jean de Luz[2]

10 *August* 1902

My dear Wells, Your book[3]—as always—has been a

[1] By 1900 eight titles by Wells had been included in the Tauchnitz series, and between 1900–05 six of his books were translated into German.

[2] Although Gissing made some recovery of strength at Arcachon, he was advised to live in the south-west of France. On April 24 he and Gabrielle moved into a chalet in St Jean de Luz at the foot of the Pyrenees. This seaside town, which had a British colony, figures in *Will Warburton*, Chapter XXXVIII. In May and June the entries in Gissing's diary remark both improvement in health and depressing idleness.

[3] *The Sea Lady*, published in August 1902, was a variation on the theme of *Love and Mr Lewisham*. In the earlier novel Lewis-

delight to me, and is now giving like pleasure to Gabrielle. Thank you heartily for your kindness in sending it.

This "tissue of moonshine"[1] is, at the same time, I take it, a substantial allegory. The allegorist, you know, is essentially an elusive person, and I do not pretend to interpret you with certainty; but what I *do* see is satisfying. That apart, the thing is daintily amusing, done with your wonted lightness of hand. I relived the strand and the cliffs in reading, and wished I could straight away take ship for your coast. Very well done (praise is here impertinent) the Bunting group; in that element you are unapproachable.

Come now; I want a successor to *Love and Mr Lewisham*. No doubt it is on the way. Speed with it.

You have heard, doubtless that brave old Hudson has a Government pension of £150.[2] Nothing for a long time has so gladdened me as the sight of that news in the *Athenaeum* a few weeks ago. For once has the right thing been done, and done in time. I feel my breathing easier since the news came; it was a physical relief. Glorious old Hudson!

---

ham's love resulted in his "domestic claustrophobia" and his necessary relinquishment of a scientific career. The hero of *The Sea Lady* escaped his fiancée and a political career by diving into the sea in search of "other dreams" represented by the mermaid.

[1] The sub-title of *The Sea Lady*.

[2] Writing to his brother on 28 December 1901 Gissing expressed the hope that "old" Hudson's friends would "not allow him to end his life in the workhouse." (*Letters of George Gissing to His Family*, p. 380.)

Long, long ago I ought to have written to Hick. Do tell him that of course it is mere midsummer negligence. He shall hear before long. I trust all goes well with him and his.

I work slowly at a novel,[1] but somehow my interest in life is not very keen. To test the state of my brain, I began 3 weeks ago to learn Spanish, and as I have just finished 16 chapters of *Don Quixote*, and can now read it quite easily, I don't think there is positive decay of mental power.[2]

It seems you have had a detestable summer in England. Here the weather has been often gloomy and cool. You must have enjoyed that Gotthard tramp![3]

All good be with you both. Our affectionate remembrances.—Is the little man flourishing?

Ever yours,

GEORGE GISSING

I should have written to James about his illness, but feared to give him the trouble of replying.

[1] Out of his need for money and his desire to create an audience, Gissing planned to make *Will Warburton* a light-hearted treatment of money and art. He began it on July 10 but had written only fifty pages by mid-October. Then he made a fresh beginning and finished it in March 1903. The book was not published until June 1905.

[2] On July 13 Gissing received from Hudson a *Spanish Dictionary and Grammar*. He spent the afternoon going through the *Grammar* and in the evening read one page of *Don Quixote*. On November 30 Gissing wrote to Clodd that he had achieved a lifelong ambition —the reading of *Don Quixote* in the original. (*Letters of George Gissing to His Family*, p. 387; Clodd, *Memories*, p. 185; *The Private Papers of Henry Ryecroft*, "Winter," XVII.)

[3] The Wellses had spent June at Lucerne and Locarno.

95

GISSING TO WELLS

26 January 1903 *Ciboure, St Jean de Luz*

MY DEAR WELLS, Yes, this is an odd situation for a retiring man.—At first glance, I took the composer of the list for a peculiarly bitter satirist, but, on reflection, I see of course that his *figures* are not meant to signify anything, and are jotted down at hazard.—At least, I hope so, or the Tasmanians are in bad case.[1]

You will receive a copy of my *Ryecroft* direct from Constable's.[2] Do not, I pray, be hurt that it comes thus, without any inscription; I am getting the publishers to send all my presentation copies, as I do not feel quite equal, just now, to the task of making up parcels and carrying them to the post. You know, I am sure, that, if I wrote in the book, it would testify to my affectionate feeling.

All goes well with you, I do not doubt. I was glad to

[1] The subject of this paragraph has eluded identification.

[2] Although the *Fortnightly Review*, which serialised *An Author at Grass*, was owned by Chapman & Hall and although Courtney, the editor, was a director of the firm, they did not purchase the book-rights. It was published in January 1903 by Archibald Constable, who advanced £100 against a royalty of twenty per cent. Constable advised that the title be changed to *The Private Papers of Henry Ryecroft*.

hear of your little flat in London.[1] If I could be *there*, I would make better use of my time than in the old days. Strange to think that there really are people who walk the streets of London. It is becoming phantasmal to me.

My kindest remembrances to Mrs Wells.

Ever yours,

GEORGE GISSING

96

GISSING TO MRS WELLS

8 *March* 1903 *Villa Lannes, Ciboure, St Jean de Luz*

DEAR MRS WELLS, Many thanks for your kindness in forwarding the letter and packet. Why Elliott & Fry should take it into their heads to send me copies of my portrait seven years late[2]—isn't it about seven years since I was at Sandgate?—I can't imagine.

Yes, H. G. had told me of the little flat. I know that corner of London, and wish I could knock joyously at your door one morning. But that will not be for a long time.

We shall be very glad to have the photograph you promise. A glimpse of the little mortal was given in your Christmas card. (I mention this, to let you know that we received the card. So many things are lost in the

[1] From December 1902 to December 1903 the Wellses lived in a flat at 6 Clement's Inn.

[2] See Letter 74.

post, and so much ill-feeling is thus caused, that I lose no opportunity of begging my correspondents never to decide harshly against me where the post *might* be to blame.)

Evans! Strange being. And yet, if his soul is satisfied with golf and bridge, why should he not go on golfing and bridging? At all events, he is working his way to sincerity.[1]

We have had a fairly good winter—more than fairly good as regards the weather. I can walk for an hour at a time, with not more than a dozen pauses to labour agonizingly for breath at the wayside. In early summer we hope to go up into the mountains, and then, if still solvent, to choose for next winter between St Jean de Luz and Amélie-les-bains, in the South-east—said to be a dry and sunny place, without mistral.

I wonder whether you see Henry James now and then. My greetings to him, please, when you do.

I await H. G's *Making of Mankind*,[2] of which unfortunately I have been able to see nothing yet. Some irresponsible scoundrel, in a column of gossip somewhere, spoke of a novel of his as all but ready;[3] I hope he for once told truth.

[1] See Letter 55, note 2.

[2] *Mankind in the Making* was published in instalments in the *Fortnightly Review*, September 1902–September 1903.

[3] The serialisation of *The Food of the Gods* began in *Pearson's Magazine*, December 1903. The book was published in September 1904.

Gabrielle wishes to be affectionately remembered to you. Do not forget my name, and believe me

Always sincerely yours,

GEORGE GISSING

97

GISSING TO G. P. WELLS [postcard]

12 *March* 1903 *Ciboure, St Jean de Luz*

Delighted to see you, and to see your father's hand—which I wish I could shake.

GEORGE GISSING

98

GISSING TO WELLS

31 *August* 1903 *Ispoure, St Jean Pied de Port, Basses Pyrénées*

MY DEAR WELLS, With my usual brutality, I have hitherto neglected to thank you for sending me a copy of the *Academy* with a notice of *Ryecroft*.[1] It was good of you;

[1] In a long and enthusiastic review the *Academy* (7 March 1903) praised Gissing in such statements as "Averse from pyrotechny of thought or phrase, he has produced books which panting fuglemen of reputation could not read while they ran." In a letter to Clodd, Gissing remarked, "It will amuse you to learn that all the noise about *Ryecroft* has hitherto resulted in a total sale which means, to me, *not quite* £200! There is literary success for you!" (Clodd, *Memories*, p. 187.)

I liked the article. Now, in the middle of my work, I grow anxious to know how you are and what you are doing. Your summer has been cheerless, they tell me; even here the rainfall is abnormal. Do you leave England for your holiday? Let me know.

A fortnight ago we spent a few days wandering in Navarre—saw the Roncesvalles of romance and the Pamplona of history—a very enjoyable little excursion. Too much evil is spoken of the Spanish food; but I should like to see the Maritornes at close quarters! She is perhaps a degree more savage than the domestic slave in Calabria. One lives (at the village inns) in awful stenches; how we escaped typhoid, I know not.

You will see from this that I am physically in better case. Since leaving St Jean de Luz (at the end of June) I have picked up wonderfully; this air of the hills suits me well. Heavens be thanked, I have done about a third of my historical novel—the 6th century story of which I spoke to you in far off Budleigh days, and which has haunted my mind for the last ten years. This time, if no ill befall me, it will be finished,[1] and I dare to think the result will not altogether displease you. I hope to have it in the hands of the brave Pinker early next year.

When do your Education papers come out in volume?[2]

[1] By early November Gissing had written two-thirds of *Veranilda*, but with the winter weather his health worsened and he never completed the novel.

[2] *Mankind in the Making* was published in September 1903.

Alas, I have seen none of them, for, as usual, I am penniless, and can buy nothing.

Conrad sent me his *Typhoon* volume, and I was delighted with it. He is a strong man.

Do you see James?—Bythebye, an English paper states that Henley died worth something more than £800.[1] Amazing! How on earth did he amass that wealth? It rejoiced me to know that his latter years have been passed without struggle for bread.

We are in a cottage amid the Pyrenees, some 30 miles inland. Around us, little but Basque is commonly spoken, though most of the people understand French. These Basques, do you know, conflict a good deal with a theory of yours which I remember, that there is practically no such thing as a distinct *race*. They have held their separate existence from the beginning of history, and still resist the influences alike of France and of Spain.

I see that Mrs Woods begins a series of articles on the Basque country in the new *Cornhill*.[2] She came to see us

[1] After W. E. Henley failed in 1895 to get the chair of English Literature in the University of Edinburgh and after the cessation in 1897 of the *New Review*, which he edited, he was awarded an annual pension of £225 by the Prime Minister, A. J. Balfour. Wells had been one of "Henley's men" on the *National Observer* and the *New Review*. Henley died on 11 July 1903.

[2] Margaret L. Woods (1856–1945), novelist, poet, and dramatist, published three articles in the *Cornhill* (1903) dealing largely with St Ignatius and the religious shrines and churches of the Basque country.

at St Jean de Luz early in the summer. A strange and rather uncanny person—with a good husband.

Tell me more of your experiences with the socially-active people. But tell me, above all, of yourselves, your work.

Gabrielle is well, reads much, and profits by this healthy life. She sends her affectionate remembrances to Mrs Wells. How goes the little man?—I hope he will not grow up under the curse of military servitude.

Every good wish to you both.

Always yours,

GEORGE GISSING

99

GISSING TO WELLS [postcard]

4 *October* 1903 *Ispoure, St Jean Pied de Port*

I am ashamed to be so long in thanking you for your book.[1] More than a week ago, I had finished it, and was about to write, when an Englishman who is here seized upon it, and he has not yet brought it back. I cannot write till I have the vol. again, for I have marked many things to speak of. Hearty thanks; you shall hear very soon. It was a good answer to my letter.—I am just past

[1] *Mankind in the Making.*

the middle of my 6th century book—gloria in excelsis! Hard, slow work.[1]

Ever yours,
G. G.

100

GISSING TO WELLS

12 *October* 1903 *Ispoure, St Jean Pied de Port*

MY DEAR WELLS, At last I have your book back, and can write about it.

Well now, with your main contention I am quite at sympathy. Seeing that mankind cannot have done altogether with the miserable mystery of life, undoubtedly it behoves us before all else to lighten as best we can the lot of those for whose being we are responsible. This for the vast majority of men. A few there are, I think, who are justified in quite neglecting that view of life, and, by-thebye, Marcus Aurelius was one of them.[2] Nothing he

[1] Although Gissing derived pleasure from the writing of *Veranilda*, he found it "harder work than any I ever did—not a line that does not ask sweat of the brain." In particular the dialogue gave him trouble. (Clodd, *Memories*, p. 191.)

[2] In *Mankind in the Making* Wells condemned the narrow, egoistic view of life which he found in most "human expression in act and art and literature." Citing the *Meditations* as an example of this "abstract and fruitless virtue," he declared "that the son of Marcus Aurelius was the unspeakable Commodus, and that the Roman Empire fell from the temporizing detachment of his rule into a century of disorder and misery."

could have done would have made Commodus other than he was, (I use, of course, everyday phrases, regardless of determinism)—and then one feels pretty sure that Commodus was not his son at all. For him, life was the individual, and, whether he has had any true influence or not, I hold him absolutely justified in thinking as he did.

Pooh! I wanted to tell you what I enjoyed in your book, and not to cavil on small points.—Yes, a thoroughly practical suggestion, that on pp. 100–1, and some day it will doubtless be carried out.[1]—Admirable your protest against slang. Pp. 128–9 tell the truth of the matter as neatly as possible,[2] and I rejoice at finding you an ally of the conservatives on this question. You were always practically so in your own writing—of which you know my opinion from of old.—I laughed with pleasure on p. 168. Capital, that explanation of the suburb "villa".[3] I had never thought of it—only wish I had

[1] In respect to the problem of neglected children Wells recommended that parents be made debtors to society for the adequate care of their offspring for twelve or thirteen years. In case of parental default the children were to be removed, and the parents were to be billed for the cost of suitable maintenance. If parents failed to pay, they were to be put in "celibate labour establishments" to work off the debt.

[2] Protesting against the poverty of vocabulary of English-speaking peoples, Wells declared that neologisms were the "stupid efforts of ignorant men to supply the unnecessary."

[3] Here Wells described a middle-class home as a fake imitation of a manor house; "it stands back a yard or so from the road, with a gate and a railing, and a patch, perhaps two feet wide, of gravel between its front and the pavement. This is the last pathetic

when I was writing of such things.—More seriously admirable are p. 186 and the following.[1] You have hit just the right tone, and told the truth in just the right words. Of course no pious Atheist will be reached by it, but what fool or ruffian was ever directly bettered by a satiric display of his folly or ruffiandom? The great thing is that those who are *just releasing* themselves from such grossness find here the help they need. It is good to preach to the converted, lest they lapse away; it is better to preach to the half-converted, for—as you rightly insist—in our time it is by reading that men's minds are formed, and everyone believes what he desires to believe.

These are passages which I have marked in satisfaction. If I had marked everything which pleased me as literature, the book would have been scored all through, for on every page there is some vigorous sentence, some

vestige of the preliminary privacies of its original type, the gates, the drive-up, the front lawn, the shady trees, that gave a great impressive margin to the door. The door has a knocker . . . and it opens into a narrow passage, perhaps four feet wide, which still retains the title of 'hall'. Oak staining on the woodwork and marbled paper accentuate the lordly memory. . . . Though the drawing-room is inevitable, the family will manage without a bathroom well enough." Readers of *The Diary of a Nobody* (1892) will recall Weedon Grossmith's satirical drawing of "The Laurels," the residence of Mr Pooter.

[1] On the problem of religious instruction Wells wished to avoid dispute, but he objected to the notion that religion, like geography, "can be got into daily lessons of one hour." He continued, "We must all agree—whatever we believe or disbelieve—that religion is the crown of the edifice we build."

ingenious phrase, some delightful novelty of utterance. Not easily nowadays will one find such a remarkable bit of word-weaving as that on p. 122, from "There will come a time" to "human mind."[1] *There* is clarity of intellect—a thing I peculiarly envy.

Nay, but you shall hear also a few objections. I fear Cope Cornford[2] is right as to early learning of foreign languages; fluency may be attained later in life, but the very accent, no; that must come when tongue, palate, lips, etc. are still growing.—On pp. 70–1, I grant you that genius is stifled a thousand times for once that it comes to fruit; but one cannot forget the law of humanity which says that all good shall be won "not without dust and heat." I fear the over-much encouraging of the

[1] "There will come a time when, at the merest touch upon those keys, image will follow image and emotion develop into emotion, when the whole creation, the deeps of space, the minutest beauties of the microscope, cities, armies, passions, splendours, sorrows, will leap out of darkness into the conscious being of thought, when this interwoven net of brief, small sounds will form the centre of a web that will hold together in its threads the universe, the All, visible and invisible, material and immaterial, real and imagined, of a human mind." Although Gissing admired this sentence, it may be suspected that it was such a passage that Wells had in mind when he later described *Mankind in the Making* as "revivalism, field preaching." (*Experiment in Autobiography*, IX, 1.)

[2] To his attack on the premature teaching of foreign languages Wells added a footnote in which he gave the opposing view of L. Cope Cornford who contended that a "particular movement of the vocal apparatus" had to be learned by the age of five or six. Cornford (1867–1927), later a naval correspondent, wrote two unusual textbooks, *English Composition* (1900) and *Essay-Writing for Schools* (1903).

young by making things easy for them—or, for that matter, of those no longer young. It is a most difficult point. On p. 128, should not you read for "a tenth part", "a thousandth part"? Do you really think that a London slave-girl possesses *a tenth* of the English language? I have known some whose vocabulary was, I swear, barely 200 words.[1]—On p. 188, are you not unjust to "dear old" Vesuvius? Surely there is a good deal of difference between a cinder-heap made by man in the pursuit of money, and a glorious mountain made by Nature in the pursuit of nothing we know of? Some of my deepest emotions have been touched, day or night, by the sight of Vesuvius. Emotions, too, I have had in the Black Country (vid. *Eve's Ransom*); but they were of another order, much as I admired the sombre beauty of what I saw.[2]—Then, that troublesome chapter on the

[1] Wells's sentence ran as follows: "I doubt if the ordinary member of the prosperous classes in England has much more than a third of the English language in use, and more than a half in knowledge, and as we go down the social scale we may come at last to strata having but a tenth part of our full vocabulary, and much of that blurred and vaguely understood."

[2] In objecting to the conventional notion that Nature consisted of certain isolated places or aspects, Wells said that Vesuvius was "grand and beautiful" whereas "the glowing cinder heaps of Burslem, the wonders of the Black Country sunset, the wonderful fire-shot nightfall of the Five Towns" were dismissed as offensive and vulgar. Gissing's descriptions of the Black Country may be found in Chapters I, IV, and XVIII of *Eve's Ransom*. His passionate admiration for Vesuvius was discussed by William Morris Colles in the *Academy* (9 January 1904).

"Imagination."[1] No, I cannot think it is practicable to have an "adult" department of publication. Heartily I agree with you when you wish to keep certain books and certain pictures out of the un-adult's way. I have always opposed the translation—e.g.—of Zola into English, seeing that everyone, without exception, capable of reading him as *literature* would take the trouble to read him in French, and only those who sought pornography would fall on the English version. But I see no way of classifying publications. Roughly, the law against obscenity rules out what should be ruled out, for old as for young; when it comes to things debatable—and remember that even such a book as Montaigne's *Essays* would have to be called "adult"—I fear humanity must go on in the old way, getting good here and evil there, each reader finding pasture or poison as his nature may be. The label "adult" would merely introduce into the world a new prurience, put in the way of the young yet one more door with the inscription "gabinétto oscéno" (as—formerly—in the Museum at Naples).

[1] In Chapter VIII, "The Cultivation of the Imagination," Wells dealt with the problem of adolescent sexual awakening and books, about which, he said, "the tragi-comic web of human absurdity thickens to its closest." With respect to complete freedom of reading for the young Wells was "on the side of the Puritans, unhesitatingly," but he was equally sure that adults should not be restricted. His answer was to price adult art and literature beyond the means of young people. Gissing's remarks to Wells may be compared with his second thoughts on prudery and verbal delicacy in *The Private Papers of Henry Ryecroft*, "Winter," XXII.

Thanks then and thanks again for this brave, upright, admirably written book. It will have great success, and will widen still more the way of your influence, which can only be for good. It has refreshed my mind, jaded a little by long brooding over my own hard bit of work. I hope you have managed a good holiday this year. Our kindest remembrances to you. When you write, send news of the little New Republican.[1]

Yours ever, my dear H. G.,

GEORGE GISSING

101

GISSING TO WELLS

27 *November* 1903 *Ispoure, St Jean Pied à Port*

MY DEAR WELLS, Your letter does me good. It is like yourself, and I thank you heartily for thinking of me in this kindly way.

But how did Pinker get hold of the idea that I was coming to England? Alas, I see no chance of it until next summer, and my ability to come even then will depend upon all sorts of things—I shall not be able to make up my mind until the last moment of possible departure. I want very badly to see England, and my friends there, but I have a lung at which doctors still look grave, and

[1] This allusion to Wells's son is a play on the title of the first chapter of *Mankind in the Making*.

several other things to make my movements very uncertain.

Please thank Mrs Wells for sending me *T.P.*[1] Yes, it is a most respectable paper—altogether above such penny weeklies as I have hitherto seen. The pile-driving chant is very curious.

Now let me speak of your book of stories.[2] I opened it with that peculiar thrill of anticipation which is given me only by your books, and the first pages of "Filmer" justified me. This kind of story is quite your own—an adaptation of the historic method altogether original with you, and resulting in a verisimilitude which no one can rival. I *like* your vivid presentment of the commonplace and its blending with the marvellous; I *like* it as I like no fiction of to-day.

[1] *T.P.'s Weekly* (20 November 1903) published a description of the labourers on the new Campanile in Venice who hoisted and released the weight of their pile-driver to the rhythm of an ancient work-song. Although there was no mention of Gissing in this issue, he had fared very well in *T.P.'s Weekly*. In the number for 26 December 1902 his abridgement of Forster's *Life of Dickens* was chosen as the "book of the week," and in the issue of 27 February 1903 *The Private Papers of Henry Ryecroft* was praised as "a book of many books."

[2] *Twelve Stories and a Dream*, published October 1903, opened with "Filmer," the first page of which declared that the mastery of flying was the work of many men but that the "inexorable injustice" of the popular mind gave the credit to a single man. The other stories referred to are "The Magic Shop," an enchanting narrative about Wells and his son Gip; "The Inexperienced Ghost," a less than successful attempt to combine comedy and the supernatural; and "Valley of Spiders," a grotesque fantasia.

Wonderful the charm of the toy-shop story; a new note, I think. Capitally done, in another way, the embarrassed phantom. Very different, again, "The Valley of Spiders"—a very curious experiment, which must, I fancy, have cost you a good deal of trouble. Well, all is good, and I rejoice in it.

My *Veranilda* is some 3/4 done, and I suppose this book, which has hovered before me so long, will this time really become a fact. I say, do you remember when we stood in the road at Budleigh Salterton, before my lodgings, talking of that? Heavens, how long ago!

I am told of a second boy.[1] All good to him! How full your life must be of work and pleasure.

Please remember us both very kindly to Mrs Wells, and believe me[2]

102

WELLS TO GOSSE[3]

4 *January* 1904 *Spade House, Sandgate, Kent*

MY DEAR GOSSE,[4] Gissing was a most amiable decent man but an absolute fool, outside the covers of a book, in

[1] Frank Richard Wells, born October 31.

[2] The signature is missing.

[3] In the upper margin of this letter are the words: "Private—except as regards the use for which the facts are given—or Barrie."

[4] Here Wells inserted an asterisk for a footnote which reads: "I'm glad you asked me." Gosse, who was seeking from Balfour a grant for the Gissing boys, asked Wells for full information.

It was natural that Gosse should apply to Wells, for the latter all arrangements and affairs, and there is nothing lurid and bad but much that is pitiful in his life. Here is the worst I know, and I think all that matters.[1]

He was a model boy at school and went to Owens College, Manchester. He did brilliantly in classics and took the first places in English and Classics at the London B.A., Intermediate Exam. But (still in his middle teens) he flamed out sexually and conceived what must have been an intense passion for a girl on the streets. He tried to keep her, there were stresses and (this is as confidential as you can keep it) one day he saw money and stole it. That's the thing that happened. He was caught, there was a police-court (don't you let this out for God's sake) and he was packed off to America. That's Gissing's crime. He got a job as private tutor to a boy, I don't know where, but I think at Boston—lost his job—went west to Chicago, where he really starved, got some work

---

was at Gissing's bedside shortly before his death. When Gissing became desperately ill just before Christmas 1903, Gabrielle sent telegrams to Wells and Morley Roberts urging them to come. On Christmas Eve Wells left for St Jean Pied de Port where he found Gissing delirious from double pneumonia. Under the impression that Roberts was to come the evening of December 27 Wells left for England that afternoon. Actually Roberts did not arrive until after Gissing's death, which occurred in the early morning of December 28.

[1] Gosse had written: "Were there not quite a number of events in his life which have to be treated gingerly?" He explained that he needed to know the worst in order not to be taken by surprise by Balfour, who was somewhat unsympathetic.

in a newspaper office, and then came back to England and *found out and married that girl of the Manchester episode.* All that, and a novel he got done before he was one and twenty. She had acquired the drink habit, she made things very bad for him, and she died in hospital of lung trouble, hardship and drink. By that time he'd got several novels out but no successes. He was very hard up and hopeless and he was fearfully oppressed by the sex necessity. I believe he was too poor for prostitutes. (This comes somewhere about the time of *New Grub Street* and the late eighties.) He read some nonsense of Lecky's about younger sons marrying girls of the lower class,[1] and he married a servant girl. He seems to have married her at a venture. There was a decent, queer life in a cottage at Exeter and then at Epsom and then she began to go mad. She had violent fits of rage, violent fits of jealousy, she ill treated her child, made work almost impossible, and he had to leave her. He got his boy away and his sisters at Wakefield (excellent women running an excellent little preparatory school) took the youngster and have done for him since, partly at Gissing's charge and partly at their own. Some idiot contrived a reconciliation with the wife, which led (and I think this is

[1] If Lecky made such a statement, it has escaped identification. In the chapter on marriage in *The Map of Life* (1899) Lecky wrote: "Probably, on the whole, the best presumption of a successful choice in marriage will be formed where the wife has not been educated in circumstances or ideas dissimilar from those of her married life."

Gissing's only other crime) to a second child. There was a second separation. Miss Orme took the wife and child into her home with the virtuous intention of civilizing her, and after the woman had threatened her with violence and taken to smashing furniture and knocking the child about, came the private asylum. Meanwhile Gissing lived alone, wandered to Italy (*By the Ionian Sea* comes here) had a home at Dorking and was finally run to earth while he was staying with me by an enterprising Frenchwoman who wanted to translate his books. She had tea with us, and seemed (as she is) a very decent intelligent woman. Afterwards she came to England again and stayed at Dorking under circumstances of extreme decorum—his mother was in the home with him at the time—and I'm fairly certain, as a commercial traveller might say, that nothing happened then. Finally misery and loneliness overtook Gissing and he went to her in Switzerland and begged her to live with him. She did—bringing a mother.[1] That happened about the time you came to look me up at New Romney, because I remember the violent rage into which a sudden unbecoming sentimentality in Gissing's letters threw me at that time. That's all. He lived with her up to the time of his death and she was a pathetic, devoted and exasperatingly incompetent nurse. It's not a story of magnificent and

[1] Here Wells inserted an asterisk calling attention to a footnote which reads: "There was of course no marriage but everyone she knew in Paris, except her mother, thought it a marriage."

artistic vice, is it? That's really every scrap I know. I think the boys ought to be provided for in the scale of his education and quality. I know it's the thing he would have asked me to try to get someone to do, if he had had strength to talk to me last week. And really I think, unless Balfour is very different from what I suppose him to be, the thing to do is just to give him the square truth.[1]

Another point in Gissing's favour is that in money matters he was a most scrupulous man. That's not so common as it might be in our profession. He was one of the most clean minded and decent of men. James by the bye has seen him—you get his impression.

Yours ever,

H. G. WELLS

103

HARRISON TO WELLS

27 *January* 1904 *Elm Hill, Hawkhurst*

DEAR MR WELLS, I think you went out to the last hours and funeral of George Gissing at St Jean. If so, I should be very glad if you could tell me something of his last

[1] Gosse gave the Prime Minister *By the Ionian Sea* and *The Private Papers of Henry Ryecroft*. Each of the boys was granted a yearly pension of £37; and in order to keep the money from falling into the hands of Mrs Edith Gissing, Balfour appointed Wells and Miss Collet as trustees. But Wells was driven to despair by Miss Collet and in July insisted upon being released from the assignment.

illness and burial. I knew him in 1884, when he sent me his *Unclassed.* I induced John Morley to read it and to give him work on the then *Pall Mall Gazette.* He was for some time, two years I think, day tutor to my two sons, and took charge of them on Ullswater when I was kept at the bedside of my wife all the summer of 1884. I knew him very well, and had a deep interest in him. He did some literary work for me at the British Museum, and I had a long and interesting letter from him when he sent me his *Henry Ryecroft.* On reading of his death in the papers, I wrote to Mrs G. Gissing. I never saw his wife. But he told my wife that she had been a farm girl, and not a woman of culture. The other day we received a very French mourning card, engraved *Madame Georges Gissing* and in a feminine *French* hand *remercîements émûs* and my name spelt Frédéric—This is a mystery. The card was not that of an English farm girl—nor was the writing or words. Had he a third French wife? Or who sent the card? I heard all about his first wife and his early life. He met an old schoolfellow at my house, and I then heard his strange sad story. Has he left a real autobiography? Have you ever seen *The Unclassed*?

Yours very truly,

FREDERIC HARRISON

104

HARRISON TO WELLS[1]

5, Rutland House, Marloes Road, W.

4 February 1904

DEAR MR WELLS, The source of the card which we received from "Madame Georges Gissing" is precisely what I supposed. Pray be under no apprehension that I should be indiscreet in the matter. This is a mere trifle—a negligible incident—in the irregular and melancholy life of our friend. I am perhaps the only living person who really knows his story, and I am glad that nothing about it will be made public—certainly not by me even to his intimate friends.

I am amused to read the various myths which his younger admirers and readers are putting about. They are mostly mere romances. George Gissing passed through a year or two of acute pressure and dreadful suffering—for which he alone was responsible. To the age of 18 he had a perfectly comfortable, easy, successful, and even brilliant life, with every prospect of a fine career. That he threw away and smarted horribly for some years. At 22 he introduced himself to me. I made him tutor to my sons. He spent every morning in my

[1] At the head of this letter are the words: "Private and Confidential."

house—he dined at my table with my sons and my wife and myself daily, came to our evening parties, and was in every sense one of our friends. I introduced him to John Morley, then Editor of the *Pall Mall Gazette*, and got Morley to employ him on the paper. This Gissing abruptly declined. I got him numerous pupils in excellent families, when my sons went to school. I sent him in charge of my family to a beautiful house on Ullswater during the autumn of 1884, which he enjoyed greatly.

He had pleasant lodgings in the Regents Park, to which my sons used to go. I gave—and offered him—introductions to editors, publishers, and could have placed in his way any amount of literary and classical engagements, and could have found him plenty of society. He had travelled much and often. Almost all of this he declined, partly perhaps owing to the horrible entanglement in which he had involved himself, partly from an incurable turn for a solitary life and the study of misery and the sordid.

The stories put about of "grinding poverty," "solitude," "hunger," "neglect," etc., etc., etc., form a myth which has grown up. 1. partly, as to 1/5th out of the acute suffering of 2 or 3 years—self-imposed. 2. partly, as to 2/5ths from the younger men assuming Henry Ryecroft and other books to be real autobiography, whereas they are romances based on detached and occasional experiences, and psychological dreams. 3. mainly—as to 2/5ths (or more) from his curious idiosyncrasy—his taste for a solitary life, and for trying what misery was like. He was a sort of amateur Fakir of modern slum life. Do not suppose that I am, or ever was, unfriendly or unsympathetic towards him. I am sure I was the most useful friend he ever had, and the one who knew him best. I understood and respected his idiosyncrasy from the first—and giving full allowance for that, I did not complain of his habit of mind so utterly alien to my own. I admired his genius though I do not rate it so high as some of his admirers. And I am sure he would have been a happier and more useful man if he had not rated his own genius as something so rare. I was on terms of the most perfect confidence and familiarity with him. And I used sometimes to rally him as being the most hardened egotist and the most refined sybarite I knew. What surprises me is that with all this roaring of the young lions about him no one seems to know his earliest and in many ways his best book—savage and foul as it is—the *Workers in the Dawn*. 4 vols.! Believe me

Very sincerely,

FREDERIC HARRISON

APPENDIX A

WELLS'S REVIEW OF *EVE'S RANSOM*[1]

THERE cannot be any question of the finished workmanship, the minute observation, the absolute truthfulness of Mr Gissing's last novel. Eve Madeley is a real and credible woman, fundamentally mean as is the way with his women, with a sweet intellectual face and an inherent refinement and seriousness that extort our respect, and with just one dash of sordid romance with a married man to vary her dull life of work and parsimony. Hilliard, again, is a subtly studied character, a mechanical draughtsman, bored to death by his monotonous life, without the energy or ability to rise or to fall tragically out of it, gradually drifting towards drunkenness as the one possible loophole from inanition. In short, he lacks nervous energy. To him comes a windfall of four hundred and thirty-six pounds. He has not the heart to attempt any sustained assault on fortune with it; he determines that he will at least "live" a couple of years, and forthwith he begins one of the dismallist raids upon pleasure that ever man made. Curiously enough, Eve, who is out of a situation in London resolves that, instead of eating up her savings slowly, she will "live" a little

[1] "The Depressed School," *Saturday Review*, 27 April 1895.

during her enforced leisure, and in a state of dreary desperation starts a round of theatres and a subscription at Mudie's. They come together—how, one must read the book to learn—and Hilliard spends the bulk of his money rescuing Eve from her melancholy intrigue with the married man by taking her to the mitigated gloom of Paris. Finally, when she is "ransomed" and his money is all spent, she throws over her ransomer for the wealthy Narramore, and attains the only happiness attainable in the world of Gissing—a red-brick villa, "rather new, of course; but a year will do wonders," no work to do, and plenty of money. And Hilliard is partly relieved at escaping the bothers of matrimony and partly exalted by the sacrifice he has made, and in the end, "a free man in his own conceit, sang to himself a song of the joy of life." With these words the book ends. After the manner of Mr. Gissing, we hear nothing of that song. These two principal characters are drawn with photographic fidelity and wonderful insight, and Patty, Eve's friend, though a much slighter sketch, is equally true; but Narramore is a mere lay figure—"energetic person with indolent habits" is the recipe for him—and his wooden quality, which might pass muster in an ordinary novel, becomes glaringly conspicuous in this grey world of conscientious veracity.

Yet is it absolute veracity? No doubt Mr Gissing's spiritual anatomy and physiology are correct, and his perspective is right; but is his colouring true? Is this harsh greyness really representative of life, even the life of the lower middle class who work for wages and are seedily respectable all their days? Does the sun never shine there, nor the wind blow from other quarters than the dry cold east? Do its people never laugh, nor weep, nor have their crowning moments of passionate outburst? Or is it that Mr Gissing is colour-blind, that he has the distinctive fault as well as the distinctive precision of photography? For our own part we do not believe that any social stratum is so dull as this melancholy world of his. Happiness is, after all, mainly a question of physical constitution: it depends mainly on one's solar plexus, and very little on one's circumstances—on the wall-paper so to speak. Given a wholesome visceral nervous system, an ugly wall-paper becomes very good fun, and a well-designed one delightful; given physiological discords, and the best wall-paper in the world becomes merely an instance of the futility of all human endeavour, and anything short of the best a bitter wrong. No doubt there are husbands like Hilliard going to and fro "muttering 'what a cursed world!' " but then there are also hundreds of men with Stevenson's constitution, taking an almost childish delight in things, dodging death as if he were a playmate, and crowning themselves with garlands. There are happy omnibus conductors, clerks delighted with their lot, workgirls having the best of times, cheerful cripples, and suicidal dukes. The true Realism, we hold, looks both on the happy and on the unhappy, interweaves some flash of joy or humour into its gloomiest tragedy. Weighed by that standard, Mr Gissing falls short. He is like Gilbert's Elderly Naval Man, "he never larks nor plays." He cannot imagine a happy marriage under a thousand a year, else you are "bored to death with worries." That horror of being hard up, the fixed idea of the dismalness of middle-class life, is not only the keynote of this book, but of all his work; it reduces it from the level of a faithful presentation of life to *genre*. It is the *genre* of nervous exhaustion, just as the Restoration drama is the *genre* of witty immorality. Only the Restoration drama was exhilarating. This is neither exhilarating nor morally helpful (like Reuben Shapcott),[1] nor terrifying, nor sedative. It is miserable. And yet we must needs admire it because it is so remarkably well done, and we must needs read it to its bitter end for the grim interest of it that never fails.

[1] The imaginary friend of Mark Rutherford and the assumed editor of *The Autobiography of Mark Rutherford* (1881).

APPENDIX B

WELLS'S REVIEW OF *THE PAYING GUEST*[1]

HERE is Mr Gissing at his best, dealing with the middle-class material he knows so intimately, and in a form neither too brief for the development of character nor too lengthy for the subtle expression of his subtle insight to grow tedious. The paying guest is a young person, "not quite the lady," who has quarrelled with her stepfather and half-sister at home; and the genteel entertainers are the Mumfords of Sutton. They are thoroughly nice people are the Mumfords, and they know the Kirby Simpsons of West Kensington and Mrs Hollings of Highgate; and, indeed, quite a lot of good people. Then there are the Fentimans—"nice people; a trifle sober, perhaps, and not in conspicuously flourishing circumstances; but perfectly presentable." The Mumfords live at Sutton, "the remoteness of their friends favoured economy; they could easily decline invitations, and need not often issue them. They had a valid excuse for avoiding public entertainments—an expense so often imposed by mere fashion." What a delightful analysis of the entire genteel spirit that last phrase implies! And they kept three servants to minister to their dignity, although enter-

[1] *Saturday Review*, 18 April 1896.

tainments were beyond their means. In the remote future, when Mr Gissing's apotheosis is accomplished, learned commentators will shake their heads over the text, well nigh incapable, in those more rational times, of understanding how these people with their one child could have been so extravagantly impecunious. Yet we, in this less happy age, know how true it is. In and about London there must be tens of thousands of Mumfords, living their stiff, little, isolated, pretentious, and exceedingly costly lives, without any more social relations with the people about them than if they were cave-dwellers, jealous, secluded, incapable of understanding the slightest departure from their own ritual, in all essentials savages still—save for a certain freedom from material brutality. Mrs Mumford's great dread was that this paying guest of hers would presently drop an aspirate; but that horror at least was spared her. But the story of the addition of the human Miss Derrick to the establishment, her reception, her troubles, and her ignominious departure, must be read to be believed. The grotesque incapacity of everyone concerned to realise for a moment her mental and moral superiority to the Mumfords is, perhaps, the finest thing in an exceedingly entertaining little volume. Why, one may ask, is it so much more entertaining than the larger novels of Mr Gissing? Mr Gissing has hitherto been the ablest, as Mr George Moore is perhaps the most prominent, exponent of what we may perhaps term the "colourless" theory of fiction.

Let your characters tell their own story, make no comment, write a novel as you would write a play. So we are robbed of the personality of the author, in order that we may get an enhanced impression of reality, and a novel merely extends the preview of the police-court reporter to the details of everyday life. The analogous theory in painting would, of course, rank a passable cyclorama above one of Raphael's cartoons. Yet so widely is this view accepted that the mere fact of a digression condemns a novel to many a respectable young critic. It is an antiquated device, say these stripling moderns, worthy only of the rude untutored minds of Sterne or Thackeray. By way of contrast and reaction, we have the new heresy of Mr Le Gallienne, who we conceive demands personality, a strutting obtrusive personality, as the sole test of literary value. Certainly the peculiar delight of this delightful little book is not in the truth of the portraiture—does not every advertising photographer exhibit your Mrs Mumford and her guest with equal fidelity at every railway station?—nor in the plausible quick sequences of events, but in the numerous faint flashes of ironical comment in the phrasing that Mr Gissing has allowed himself. We congratulate Mr Gissing unreservedly on this breaking with an entirely misleading, because entirely one-sided, view of the methods of fiction. Thus liberated, his possibilities widen. Mr Gissing has an enviable part as a novelist; a steady conquest of reviewers is to his credit. He has shown beyond all denial an amazing gift of restraint, a studious avoidance of perceptible wit, humour, or pathos that appealed irresistibly to their sympathies. Now if he will let himself go, which he may do with impunity, and laugh and talk and point with his finger and cough to hide a tear, and generally assert his humanity, he may even at last conquer the reading public.

APPENDIX C

"THE NOVELS OF MR GEORGE GISSING"[1]

by H. G. Wells

In the general acceptation and in the spirit of most reviewing, a cheerful alacrity of story, together with certain grammatical observances, are apparently the end of the novelist's art. It is, no doubt, the most obvious function of the novel of commerce, that it should fill, if possible without resort to split infinitives, the gaps where the texture of unadventurous lives thins out to the blankly uneventful. But if the novel is to be treated as literature, it must rise unmistakably above this level of bogus gossip entertainingly told. Tried by the lower standard, it is doubtful if the novels of Mr Gissing would procure him a favourable verdict; it is said they are "depressing"—a worse fault surely even than "unreadableness." But in the study, at any rate, they are not so lightly dismissed. Whatever their value as pastime, it is undeniable that so soon as Mr Gissing's novels are read with a view to their structural design and implications they become very significant literature indeed.

The earlier novelists seem to have shaped their stories

[1] *Contemporary Review*, August 1897.

almost invariably upon an illustrative moral intention, and to have made a typical individual, whose name was commonly the title of the novel, the structural skeleton, the sustaining interest of the book. He or she was presented in no personal spirit; Tom Jones came forward in the interests of domestic tolerance, and the admirable Pamela let the light of restraint shine before her sex. Beauty of form does not seem to have been sought by the earlier novelists—suffice it if the fabric cohered. About the central character a system of reacting personages and foils was arranged, and the whole was woven together by an ingenious and frequently complicated "plot." The grouping is at its simplest and best in the gracefully constructed novels of Jane Austen. As the novel developed in length under the influence of periodical publication, the need of some sustaining structure of ampler dimensions than the type individual led to the complications of "plot" to hold the bulk together. Plot grew at last to be the curse of English fiction. One sees it in its most instructive aspect in the novels of Dickens, wherein personages, delightfully drawn, struggle like herrings in a net amidst the infinite reticulations of vapid intrigue. Who forgets Mr Smallweed, and who remembers what he had to do with Lady Dedlock's secret? And in the novels of Wilkie Collins the plot in its direst form tramples stark and terrible. But in the novels of Dickens there also appears another structural influence. As Poe admirably demonstrated, the "plot" of *Barnaby Rudge* collapsed under its weight of characters, and the Gordon riots were swept across the complications of the story. The new structural conception was the grouping of characters and incidents, no longer about a lost will, a hidden murder, or a mislaid child, but about some social influence or some far-reaching movement of humanity. Its first great exponent was Victor Hugo, as Stevenson insists in one of his all too rare essays, and in the colossal series of Balzac each novel aims to render a facet in the complex figure of a modern social organisation. Zola's *Lourdes* and *Rome*, and Tolstoi's *War and Peace* are admirable examples of this impersonal type of structure. This new and broader conception of novel construction finds its most perfect expression in several of the works of Turgenev, in *Smoke*, for instance, and *Virgin Soil*, each displaying a group of typical individuals at the point of action of some great social force, the social force in question and not the "hero" and "heroine" being the real operative interest of the story.

No English novelists of the first rank have arisen to place beside the great Continental masters in this more spacious development of structural method. The unique work of Mr Meredith and the novels of Mr Hardy are essentially novels of persons, freed from the earlier incubus of plot. Diana and Ethelberta, Sir Willoughby Patterne and Jude, are strongly marked individuals and only casually representative. In the novels of Disraeli —in *Sybil*, for example—political forces appear, but scarcely as operative causes, and George Eliot and Mrs Humphry Ward veil a strongly didactic disposition under an appearance of social study rather than give us social studies. Within the last few years, however, three English novelists at least have arisen, who have set themselves to write novels which are neither studies of character essentially, nor essentially series of incidents, but deliberate attempts to present in typical groupings distinct phases of our social order. And of these the most important is certainly Mr George Gissing.

The Whirlpool, for instance, Mr Gissing's latest novel, has for its structural theme the fatal excitement and extravagance of the social life of London; Rolfe, Carnaby, Alma, Sybil, Redgrave, and Mrs Strangeways are, in the first place, floats spinning in the eddy. The book opens with the flight of the insolvent Wager, leaving his children to the landlady's tender mercies, and broadens to the vivid contrast of the suicide of Frothingham in his office, while his home is crowded with a multitudinous gathering of the semi-fashionable. The interlacing threads of the story weave steadily about this theme. Rolfe marries Alma, and for a couple of years they live an ostentatiously simple life in Wales, only to feel the fatal attraction grow stronger, and come circling back at last towards the vortex. Carnaby and his wife wander abroad seeking phantasmal fortunes for a space, but the fortune does not come and the exile becomes unendurable. Sooner or later the great eddy of strenuous vanity drags them all down (saving only Rolfe) to shame and futility, to dishonour and misery, or to absolute destruction. The design has none of the spare severity that makes the novels of Turgenev supreme, but the breadth and power of its conception are indisputable. It is, perhaps, the most vigorously designed of all the remarkable series of novels Mr Gissing has given us. But the scheme of his *Emancipated* is scarcely less direct, presenting as it does, in an admirably contrived grouping, the more or less complete release from religious and moral restraints of a number of typical characters. *In the Year of Jubilee* is more subtly and less consistently planned. The picture of lower middle-class barbarism, relieved by the appreciative comments of Mr Samuel Barmby, voracious reader of a latter-day press, was conceived in a fine vein of satire, but the development of the really very unentertaining passions of the genteel Tarrant robs the book of its unity and it breaks up into a froth of intrigue about a foolish will and ends mere novel of a very ordinary kind. But Samuel Barmby, with his delightful estimate of progress by statistics, the savage truthfulness in the treatment of the French sisters, the description of Nancy's art furnishing, the characters of Horace Lord and Crewe, atone for a dozen Tarrants.

So far as the structural scheme goes there is an increased conventionality of treatment as we pass to Mr Gissing's earlier novels, to *Thyrza*, *Demos*, and *The Nether World*, and from these the curious may descend still lower to the amiable renunciations in *A Life's Morning*. *The Unclassed* has its width of implication mainly in its name; it is a story of by no means typical persons, and with no evident sense of the larger issues. But *The Nether World*, for instance, albeit indisputably "plottesque," and with such violent story mechanisms in it as the incredible Clem Peckover and that impossible ancient, Snowdon, does in its title, and here and there in a fine passage, betray already an inkling of the spacious quality of design the late works more and more clearly display. Witness the broad handling of such a passage as this:

"With the first breath of winter there passes a voice half-menacing, half-mournful, through all the barren ways and phantom-haunted refuges of the nether world. Too quickly has vanished the brief season when the sky is clement, when a little food suffices, and the chances of earning that little are more numerous than at other times; this wind that gives utterance to its familiar warning is the *avant-courier* of cold and hunger and solicitude that knows not sleep. Will the winter be a hard one? It is the question that concerns this world before all others, that occupies alike the patient work-folk who have yet their home unbroken, the strugglers foredoomed to loss of such scant needments as the summer gifted them withal, the hopeless and the self-abandoned and the lurking creatures of prey. To all of them the first chill breath from a lowering sky has its voice of admonition: they set their faces, they sigh, or whisper a prayer, or fling out a curse, each according to his nature."

The treatment of the work of Mr Gissing as a progress, an adolescence, is inevitable. In the case of no other important writer does one perceive quite so clearly the steady elimination of immaturities. As a matter of fact his first novels must have been published when he was ridiculously young. I cannot profess research in this matter, but a raid upon dates brings to light the fact that a novel—it is unnecessary to give the curious the title—was published before 1881. It was long, so long that a year, at least, must have gone in the writing of it. And a convenient compendium of literary details informs me that in this year of grace 1897 Mr Gissing is thirty-nine years old. This helps one to observe, what is still apparent without this chronological assistance, that he has been learning life and his art simultaneously. Very few novels indeed, of any literary value, have been written by men below thirty. Work essentially imaginative or essentially superficial a man of three and twenty may do as well as a man of forty; romance of all sorts, the fantastic story, the idealistic novel, even the novel of manners; all these are work for the young, perhaps even more than the old. But to see life clearly and whole, to see and represent it with absolute self-detachment, with absolute justice, above all with evenly balanced sympathy, is an ambition permitted only to a man full grown. It is the consequence of, it is the compensation for, the final strippings of disillusionment. "There am I among the others," the novelist must say, "so little capable, a thing of flimsy will, undisciplined desires and fitful powers, shaped by these accidents and driving with the others to my appointed end." And until that serene upland of despair, that wide and peaceful viewpoint is reached, men must needs be partisans, and whatever their resolves may be, the idealising touch, the partiality, the inevitable taint of justification, will mar their handiwork.

Through all the novels of Mr Gissing, fading with their progress, indeed, and yet still evident even in the latest, runs this quality of bias, that intervention. Very few of them are without a "most favoured" character. In *The Whirlpool* Rolfe plays the chief sympathetic part. Contrasted with the favoured characters of the earlier works he is singularly inert, he flickers into a temporary vitality to marry, and subsides; his character persists unchanging through a world of change. The whole design is an attraction, a disastrous vortex, but he survives without an effort; he remains motionless and implies fundamental doubts. He reflects, he does not react. He has, in fact, all the distinctive inhumanities of what one might call the "exponent character," the superior commentary. If he errs he errs with elaborate conscientiousness; in all the petty manifestations of humanity, irritability, glimpses of vanity, casual blunders and stupidities, such details as enrich even the most perfect of real human beings, he is sadly to seek. Beside such subtle, real and significant characters as the brilliantly analysed Alma, Hugh Carnaby and his wife, Buncombe, Felix Dymes and Morphew, he gives one something of the impression one would receive on getting into an omnibus and discovering a respectably dressed figure of wax among the passengers. But Rolfe is but the survivor of a primordial race in the Gissing universe; like the ornithorhyncus he represents a vanishing order. Personages of this kind grow more important, more commanding, more influential in their inhuman activities, as one passes towards the earlier works, and to compare Rolfe to Waymark (of *The Unclassed*) and that eloquent letter-writer, Egremont, in *Thyrza*, is to measure a long journey towards the impersonal in art. In *The Nether World* there are among such indubitable specimens of the kindly race of men as Pennyloaf and the Byasses, not only "good characters" but "bad" also. The steady emancipation is indisputable.

In one little book at least, *The Paying Guest*, published about a twelvemonth ago, the exponent personage has no place; so that is, indeed, in spite of its purely episodical character, one of the most satisfactory of Mr Gissing's books. It presents in a vein of quiet satire, by no means unfeeling, and from a standpoint entirely external, the meagre pretentiousness of a small suburban villa, the amazing want of intelligence which cripples middle-class life. It is compact of admirable touches. The villa was at Sutton, so conveniently distant from London that "they had a valid excuse for avoiding public entertainments—

an expense so often imposed by mere fashion." And while the negotiations for the Paying Guest were in progress, "at this moment a servant entered with tea, and Emmeline, sorely flurried, talked rapidly of the advantages of Sutton as a residence. She did not allow her visitor to put in a word till the door closed again." These are haphazard specimens of the texture. Their quality is the quality of Jane Austen, and whenever in the larger books the youthful intensity of exposition, the stress of deliberate implications relaxes, the same delicate subtlety of humour comes to the surface. Nearest to *The Paying Guest*, in this emancipation from the idealising stress, come that remarkable group of three figures, *Eve's Ransom*, and the long novel of *New Grub Street*.

Apart from their aspect as a diminishing series of blemishes, of artistic disfigurements, the "exponent" characters of Mr Gissing deserve a careful consideration. If they are, in varying proportion, ideal personages, unstudied invention that is, they are, at any rate, unconventional ideal persons, created to satisfy the author rather than his readers. Taken collectively, they present an interesting and typical development, they display the personal problem with a quality of quite unpremeditated frankness. In that very early novel, *The Unclassed*, the exponent character is called Waymark, but, indeed, Egremont, Quarrier, Ross Mallard, Tarrant, and Rolfe are all, with a varying qualification of irony, successive Waymarks. At the outset we encounter an attitude of mind essentially idealistic, hedonistic, and polite, a mind coming from culture to the study of life, trying life, which is so terrible, so brutal, so sad and so tenderly beautiful, by the clear methodical measurements of an artificial refinement, and expressing even in its earliest utterance a note of disappointment. At first, indeed, the illusion dominates the disappointment. *The Unclassed* is still generous beyond the possibilities of truth. It deals with the "daughters of joy," the culinary garbage necessary, as Mr Lecky tells us, to the feast of English morality; and it is a pathetic endeavour to prove that these poor girls are —young ladies. Jane Snowdon, the rescued drudge in *The Nether World*, Mr Gissing's parallel to the immortal Marchioness, falls short of conviction from the same desire to square reality to the narrow perfections of a refined life. She is one of nature's young ladies, her taste is innate. She often laughs, but "this instinct of gladness had a very different significance from the animal vitality which prompted the constant laughter of Bessie Byass; it was but one manifestation of a moral force which made itself nobly felt in many another way." The implicit classification of this sentence is the essential fallacy of Mr Gissing's earlier attitude:—there are two orders of human beings. It is vividly apparent in *Thyrza*. It is evident in a curious frequency of that word "noble" throughout all his works. The suburban streets are ignoble, great London altogether is ignoble, the continent of America also, considered as a whole. This nobility is a complex conception of dignity and space and leisure, of wide, detailed, and complete knowledge, of precision of speech and act without flaw or effort; it is, indeed, the hopeless ideal of a scholarly refinement.

As one passes to the later novels the clearness of vision increases, and the tone of disappointment deepens. *The Emancipated* is a flight to Italy to escape that steady disillusionment. People say that much of Mr Gissing's work is "depressing," and to a reader who accepts his postulates it is indisputable that it is so. The idealised "noble" women drop out of these later works altogether, the exponent personages no longer marry and prosper, but suffer, and their nobility tarnishes. Yet he clings in the strangest way to his early standards of value, and merely widens his condemnation with a widening experience. In *Eve's Ransom* and *New Grub Street* the stress between an increasingly truthful vision of things and the odd, unaltered conception that life can only be endurable with leisure, with a variety of books, agreeable furniture, service, costume, and refined social functions, finds its acute expression. The exponent character—a very human one—in *New Grub Street*, Reardon, is killed by that conflict, and the book ends in irony.

" 'Happiness is the nurse of virtue," said Jasper.

" 'And independence the root of happiness,' answers Amy.

" 'True. "The glorious privilege of being independent"—yes, Burns understood the matter. Go to the piano, dear, and play me something. If I don't mind, I shall fall into Whelpdale's vein, and talk about my "blessedness." Ha! Isn't the world a glorious place?'

" 'For rich people.'

" 'Yes, for rich people. How I pity the poor devils!—Play anything. Better still if you will sing, my nightingale!'

"So Amy first played, and then sang, and Jasper lay back in dreamy bliss."

So ends *New Grub Street* with the ideal attained—at a price. But that price is still only a partial measure of the impracticability of the refined ideal. So far, children have played but a little part in Mr Gissing's novels. In *The Whirlpool*, on the other hand, the implication is always of the children, children being neglected, children dying untimely, children that are never born. *The Whirlpool* is full of the suggestion of a view greatly widened, and to many readers it will certainly convey the final condemnation of a "noble" way of life which, as things are, must necessarily be built on ignoble expedients. Mrs Abbott's room, "A very cosy room, where, amid books and pictures, and by a large fire, the lady of the house sat reading Ribot," would surely have been the room of one of the most exemplary characters in the days before *New Grub Street*. But the new factor comes in with, "She had had one child; it struggled through a few months of sickly life, and died of convulsions during its mother's absence at a garden party." In the opening chapter, moreover,

Rolfe speaks of children, putting the older teaching into brutal phrases:

"They're a burden, a hindrance, a perpetual source of worry and misery. Most wives are sacrificed to the next generation—an outrageous absurdity. People snivel over the death of babies; I see nothing to grieve about. If a child dies, why, the probabilities are it *ought* to die; if it lives, it lives, and you get the survival of the fittest."

The fashionable, delightful, childless Sybil "hates housekeeping." And Alma, pursuing the phantom of a career as a musical genius, leaves for the future one little lad, "slight, and with little or no colour in his cheeks, a wistful, timid smile on his too-intelligent face." In the early novels it would seem that the worst evil Mr Gissing could conceive was crudity, passion, sordidness and pain. But *The Whirlpool* is a novel of the civilised, and a countervailing evil is discovered—sterility. This brilliant refinement spins down to extinction, it is the way of death. London is a great dying-place, and the old stupidities of the homely family are, after all, the right way. That is *The Whirlpool*'s implication, amounting very nearly to a flat contradiction of the ideals of the immature *Emancipated*. The widowed Mrs Abbott, desolate and penitent, gets to work at the teaching of children. And finally we come on this remarkable passage:

"It was a little book called *Barrack-Room Ballads*. Harvey read it here and there, with no stinted expression of delight, occasionally shouting his appreciation. Morton, pipe in mouth, listened with a smile, and joined more moderately in the reader's bursts of enthusiasm.

" 'Here's the strong man made articulate,' cried Rolfe at length. 'It's no use; he stamps down one's prejudice. It's the voice of the reaction. Millions of men, natural men, revolting against the softness and sweetness of civilisation; men all over the world, hardly knowing what they want and what they don't want; and here comes one who speaks for them—speaks with a vengeance.'

" 'Undeniable.'

" '*But*——.

" 'I was waiting for the *but*,' said Morton, with a smile and a nod.

" 'The brute savagery of it! The very lingo—how appropriate it is! The tongue of Whitechapel blaring lust of life in the track of English guns. He knows it; the man is a great artist; he smiles at the voice of his genius. It's a long time since the end of the Napoleonic wars. We must look to our physique, and make ourselves ready. Those Lancashire operatives, laming and killing each other at football, turning a game into a battle. Women turn to cricket—tennis is too soft—and to-morrow they'll be bicycling by the thousand; they must breed a stouter race. We may reasonably hope, old man, to see our boys blown into small bits by the explosive that hasn't got its name yet.'

" 'Perhaps,' replied Morton meditatively. 'And yet there are considerable forces on the other side.'

" 'Pooh! The philosopher sitting on the safety-valve. He has breadth of beam, good, sedentary man, but when the moment comes—— The Empire; that's beginning to mean something. The average Englander has never grasped the fact that there was such a thing as a British Empire. By God! we are the British Empire, and we'll just show 'em what *that* means!'

" 'I'm reading the campaigns of Belisarius,' said Morton, after a pause.

" 'What has that to do with it?'

" 'Thank heaven, nothing whatever.'

" 'I bore you,' said Harvey, laughing. 'Morphew is going to New Zealand. I had a letter from him this morning. Here it is. "I heard yesterday that H. W. is dead. She died a fortnight ago, and a letter from her mother has only just reached me in a roundabout way. I know you don't care to hear from me, but I'll just say that I'm going out to New Zealand. I don't know what I shall do there, but a fellow has asked me to go with him, and it's better than rotting here. It may help me to escape the devil yet; if so, you shall hear. Good-bye!" '

"He thrust the letter back into his pocket.

" 'I rather thought the end would be pyrogallic acid.'

" 'He had the good sense to prefer ozone,' said Morton."

Of course Rolfe here is not Mr Gissing, but quite

evidently his speeches are not a genuinely objective study of opinions expressed. The passage is essentially a lapse into "exposition." The two speakers, Morton and Rolfe, become the vehicles of a personal doubt, taking sides between the old idea of refined withdrawal from the tumult and struggle for existence, and the new and growing sense of the eternity and universality of conflict; it is a discussion, in fact, between a conception of spacious culture and a conception of struggle and survival. In his previous books Mr Gissing has found nothing but tragedy and the condemnation of life in the incompatibility between the refined way of life and life as it is. But here, in the mouth of a largely sympathetic character, is a vigorous exposition of the acceptance, the vivid appreciation of things as they are.

Enough has been written to show that *The Whirlpool* is a very remarkable novel, not only in its artistic quality, but in its presentation of a personal attitude. The clear change in the way of thinking that Mr Gissing's Rolfe is formulating (while the Whirlpool should be devouring him) is no incidental change of one man's opinion, it is a change that is sweeping over the minds of thousands of educated men. It is the discovery of the insufficiency of the cultivated life and its necessary insincerities; it is a return to the essential, to honourable struggle as the epic factor in life, to children as the matter of morality and the sanction of the securities of civilisation.

To those who are familiar with Mr Gissing's work, the

conviction that this character of Rolfe marks a distinct turning-point in his development will be inevitable. That his next work will be more impersonal than any that have gone before, that the characteristic insistence on what is really a personal discontent will be to some extent alleviated, seems to me, at any rate, a safe prophecy. Mr Gissing has written a series of extremely significant novels, perhaps the only series of novels in the last decade whose interest has been strictly contemporary. And even this last one, it seems to me, has still the quality of a beginning. It is by reason of his contemporary quality, by virtue of my belief that, admirable as his work has been, he is still barely ripening and that his best has still to come, that I have made this brief notice rather an analysis of his peculiarities and the tendencies of his development than the essay I could write with ease and sincerity in his praise.

APPENDIX D

GEORGE GISSING: AN IMPRESSION

by H. G. Wells[1]

THE tragic accident, for such the last sudden illness of George Gissing must be accounted, that leaves *Veranilda*, his long-contemplated romance, incomplete, renders it not only seemly but necessary that there should be some brief introductory presentation of the spirit in which it was conceived. Through most of the life he led as a widely respected, but never very popular or prosperous writer, there existed the strangest misconceptions of his personal quality, and he was figured as the embodiment of nearly everything he most disliked. Because he exhausted the resources of a fine irony upon the narrowness and sordidness of contemporary life, a public incapable of irony conceived him as sordid and narrow; because he was possessed by so passionate a preference for the legend of classical Rome that all modern life was colourless and insignificant in his eyes, an eminent interviewer could, as his mortuary chaplet, fling out a condescending and regretful condemnation of his "modern-

[1] Originally written as a preface to *Veranilda*, but rejected by Gissing's family; published in the *Monthly Review*, August 1904.

ity"; and he whose whole life was one unhappiness because he would not face realities, was declared the master and leader of the English realistic school. He has been likened to Zola, a well-nigh incredible feat of criticism; and a legend of him as a prowling figure gathering "copy"—they always call it "copy"—"among the barrows of East End costermongers," and in the galleries of "slum side theatres," has been the imaginative response to this illuminating comparison. His life and these inventions lie patent for the Griswolds[1] of our time; and there is the clear possibility of an English parallel to that cairn of misrepresentation and ugly falsehood which the Americans have deemed a fitting monument to their Poe. For the proper reading of *Veranilda*, if for no other reason, this growing legend must be resolutely thrust aside.

For the beginning of a juster picture there can be nothing better than the figure of Gissing as a schoolboy, obsessed by a consuming passion for learning, at the Quakers' boarding-school at Alderley Edge. He had come thither from Wakefield at the age of thirteen, and after the death of his father, who was in a double sense the cardinal formative influence in his life. The tones of his father's voice, his father's gestures, never departed from him; when he read aloud, particularly if it was poetry he read, his father returned in him. He could

[1] Rufus W. Griswold (1815–57), journalist and anthologist, wrote a notoriously hostile memoir of Edgar Allan Poe.

draw in those days with great skill and vigour—it will seem significant to many that he was particularly fascinated by Hogarth's work, and that he copied and imitated it—and his father's well-stocked library and his father's encouragement had quickened his imagination and given it its enduring bias for literary activity. One sees him at Alderley Edge as a rather pale and slightly hollow-cheeked boy, the eldest and most zealous of three brothers, who were all redoubtable workers. The school, though socially unpretentious, was a good one. Its head-master, Mr James Wood, was something of an enthusiast; and Gissing, whose imagination may have been quickened by the recent death of his father, and by a clear knowledge of the effort his education cost, seems to have flung himself at his opportunities with an almost exaggerated intensity. He joined as little as possible in the school games—though he played hockey, an old school-fellow witnesses, with "madness and vigour"—and he walked much alone. For the rest, he worked. He would work even at his exercise, reading as he walked. Occasionally his imagination and energy found vent in the violent bouts of tilting and the Greek, French, or English play performed on the half-yearly speech nights was a great thing for him. "Gissing," that old school-fellow writes, "was our shining light. He was at one and the same time, stage builder, stage manager, instructor, leading actor and prompter, as well as our chief reciter." Except in the enthusiasm of such enterprises, he seems to have had noticeably little companionship with the mass of his schoolfellows. He was speedily the prodigy of the school, a lonely prodigy, living overmuch among books, already out of touch with life, and already possessed by

> The glory that was Greece
> And the grandeur that was Rome

that were his standards throughout all the rest of his life.

He finished school prodigiously—measured by the scale of his school. He came out first of the kingdom in the Oxford Local Examination, and carried the same unqualified energy of study to Owens College, where for a time his story was an unbroken record of prize-winning. He was not quite fifteen when he entered the college, and at the end of his first session he gained Professor Wood's English Poem Prize, as well as a special prize and exhibition for classics. He also won the Shakespeare Scholarship. He worked as youngsters of his type will—insanely. He worked while he ate, he cut down his sleep, and for him the penalty came not in a palpable, definable illness, but in an abrupt, incongruous reaction and collapse. He truncated his career at Owens, with his degree incomplete—he had already taken the first place in first-class honours for English and classics in the University of London at the Intermediate Examination in Arts—and from that time his is a broken and abnormal career. He fancied he had cut himself off by this deflection from that clear course to a learned distinction which his quality and inclination alike indicated for him. He crossed to America, and was for a short time a classical tutor in Boston. He threw up his position on some forgotten ground, and went in the vaguest spirit to Chicago. There he began to show still more clearly that practical incapacity, that curious inability to do the sane, secure thing which is the hidden element in his career. It is not that he was a careless man, he was a most careful one; it is not that he was a morally lax man, he was almost morbidly the reverse. Neither was he morose or eccentric in his motives or bearing; he was genial, conversational, and well-meaning. But he had some sort of blindness towards his fellow men, so that he never entirely grasped the spirit of everyday life, so that he, who was so copiously intelligent in the things of the study, misunderstood, blundered, was nervously diffident, and wilful and spasmodic in common affairs, in employment and buying and selling, and the normal conflicts of intercourse. He did not know what would offend, and he did not know what would please. He irritated others and thwarted himself. He had no social nerve. In Chicago he came near to absolute starvation. And there it was that, with some journalistic fiction, quite lost to the world, his career of print began; though, of course, he had written much both of verse and prose before that time. He was nearly twenty.

He returned to London. By this time he had discovered what was not so much an artistic impulse as an ill-advised ambition to write a series of novels. He set to work with the enthusiasm of his nature; he worked, he wrote to his sister, "with fervour and delight"; but indeed these creations were not his own true expression. That time, twenty years ago, was an epoch, of which we perhaps are seeing the closing years, in which there was no way to distinction in art save to paint the great pretentious subject-picture in oils, the Royal Academy picture, of which the Tate Gallery is the fitting mausoleum, and in letters, outside journalism, there was no other form than the big novel to which a young man could resort and hope to live. The air was full of the successes of novelists, of their clamorous and as yet incompletely vulgarised fame. And when we examine the triumphs of that period, it is not wonderful that Gissing should have embarked upon this enterprise with a confidence that was within sight of arrogance. He had in his folly turned his back upon learning, and here was his second opportunity. He had a genuine love and admiration for Dickens, and the story of Balzac's indomitable industry must have had a singular appeal to him. In the "three sous for bread, two for milk, and three for firing," in the incessant toil and the nocturnal wanderings of that giant, there lay a snare for George Gissing's imagination. He would in those days say of so and so, "How can he write?—he has never starved!" More or less deliberately he set himself to the scheme of an English *Comédie Humaine*, and in the very titles of such novels as *The Unclassed*, *The Nether World*, *The Emancipated*, and *The Whirlpool*, lurks the faint aroma of his examplar. He must have set his course to this determination before he was twenty-one, and it was surely the most unhappy and presumptuous of undertakings. His knowledge of the world was strangely limited, was scarcely existent; home life at Wakefield was the most living thing in it, and beyond that there were school days and college passed in a dream of bookish study, some experiences in America too disagreeable for use, and now this return to London, and, until the fame accrued, tuition. The world he set himself to draw was stranger to him by far than the Rome and the Athens his books had made real to him, and the silent factor of his own quality, that, too, was undetermined. But he trusted in his strength; he trusted to the same energy and powers of devotion that had made him a prodigy at Alderley Edge and Owens College, to make him a prodigy in letters.

It is well to attempt some pictures of him at this stage. His boyhood of study had neither dwarfed nor disfigured him, and he was then a figure of youth, vigour, and promise. He was of rather more than average stature, finely proportioned, and save for a droop of the shoulders and that slight failure from grace that neglect of exercise entails, he carried himself well. His head was finely formed, and though he was spare, his skin was well seeming, and he had in his flushed moments the ruddy English colour. His features were clear cut and regular, his eyes dark blue, and his hair, which was brown with a pleasing reddish tinge, flowed back from his forehead very handsomely. He had quite distinctly a presence. His voice was sound and full, and a youth in which books had overstopped experience had made his diction more bookish and rotund than common. He was at first a little shy in intercourse, but then intelligent, self-forgetful, inaggressive, and enthusiastic. He must have seemed, he did seem, to those who met him in those days, a man of the richest possibilities.

Yet the same insidious weakness, at the point where imagination and thought pass into action, had already, behind this front of promise, contrived an arrangement of absurdities. He occupied a flat near Regents Park, and he moved in cultivated society. He had such friends as Mr Frederic Harrison, whose sons he instructed in Greek, and who was assiduous in his interest. He entered spheres in which bishops' wives are not unknown, and he has described to the present writer a conversation upon the decay of butlers with one of these ladies. She asked him how *he* managed. But, indeed, he dispensed with a butler's attentions. It will be incredible to every level-minded reader, but, as a matter of fact, he maintained this fair appearance, he received his pupils in his apartment, he toiled and wrote unceasingly, upon scarcely any food at all. Partly, no doubt, it was poverty: he grudged every moment taken by teaching from his literary purpose, and taught as little as he could; but mainly it was sheer inability to manage. His meals were of bread and dripping, stewed tea, cheese at times, soup bought desiccated in penny packets, and suchlike victual; and a common friend, himself no mean novelist, has described his entertainment there of a Sunday afternoon;—Gissing, with flushed face and shining eyes, declaiming Greek choruses and capping sonorous quotations—"There are miserable wretches," he would say, "who know not the difference between dochmiacs and antipaests!"—until hunger could wait no longer. Thereupon he would become spasmodically culinary in a swift anti-climax: "Now for the squalid meal!"

Periods of far too intense literary activity would alternate with phases of exhaustion. And only those who have passed through the moral and imaginative strain of sustained creative work will fully imagine the sense of discomfort, the realisation of loneliness that must have characterised these interludes. To the sympathetic reader who knows *New Grub Street*, *The Crown of Life*, and the earlier novels, little further is needed for the full understanding of Gissing's early manhood. There were misadventures; there was a rash, unhappy marriage; but the real stuff of his waking life was the steady flow of writing that was to be that misconceived series of novels. From first to last in that endeavour he wrote in his minute, clear hand, writing always with the full available power of his attention, nearly two million words. An hour's experiment in original composition, a little counting and a little computation brings home to one what that means. This brief paper, for example, has consumed all a man's energies for four full days. For one who writes for anything but commercial ends, this grey of written paper is the text of life, the reality of his emotions and his imagination; the other things are indeed no more than margin to that. So he wrote. He wrote for the most part about people he disliked or despised, and about people he did not understand; about social conditions that seemed to him perverse and stupid, and about ways of life into which he had never entered. He wrote with a declining belief in his own power, with a failing hope of appreciation and applause, and too often without any joy in the writing. There were quite tragic incidents, books begun and destroyed. In view of his quality it was unavoidable that much that he wrote should be considerable; and there are in all these novels eloquent passages, tender passages, passages of free and happy humour, and a pervading irony that will certainly secure them a permanent, though perhaps a dusty place, in the storehouse of English literary achievement. But there are great uninspired intervals across which the pen has been driven grimly, insistently; factitious characters evolved from his own inner consciousness, and for all his wariness and dexterity, incurably unconvincing; incompatibilities and impossibilities, and grey, tired places. And indeed, for all their merit and value, when one thinks of the middle years of this man's life—of journeys and relationships and hopes, and this and that—it all seems to be going on under a sunless sky, across which this grey cloud canopy, this unending, inky succession of words, drives remorselessly forever.

He was hidden from the light of himself. Sometimes this work welkin is tedious and impenetrable, like the cloud drift of a melancholy day; sometimes it grows thin, and a gleam of personality strikes down to warm the reader, and then one says, "This is not toil; this is Gissing." But for the most part the man is altogether masked by that premature, overwhelming intention. Behind that, unsuspected by all who did not know him, the light of classical enthusiasms that had lit his boyhood was hidden. There came a season when he had a success, when some early novel—*Demos*, if I am not mistaken—brought money, fifty pounds or so, to hand. He paid small heed then to those back street researches, those gutter-smellings the popular legend of him requires; he went straight by sea to the land of his dreams, Italy. It was still happily before the enterprise of touring agencies had robbed the idea of Italian travel of its last vestiges of magic. He spent as much time as he could afford about the Bay of Naples, and then came on with a rejoicing heart to Rome—Rome whose topography had been with him since boyhood, beside whose stately history the confused tumult of the contemporary newspaper seemed to him no more than a noisy, unmeaning persecution of the mind. Afterwards he went to Athens. But he wrote nothing of the reality of his sensations then. The self-imposed obligation of those novels weighed him down, and in *The Emancipated*, one of his least successful books, his enthusiasm seeks and fails to find expression. Within a very little of that journey, he began definitely to face the fact of his false start and to turn his mind to the discovery of his proper medium. It is at least ten years since the project of his great romance of the Gothic kingdom had definitely formed in his mind. He had written then to his home, of something fresh that was coming, of a romance that was to be altogether a break from his established style of work, and from that day to this he has held himself persistently to this plan, reading for it, scheming for it, and dreaming of it. Only the labour of writing it remained at last, and that was begun too late.

Two of his friends spent a spring-time holiday with him and his sister at Budleigh Salterton in 1897. He was then no longer the glorious, indefatigable, impracticable youth of the London flat, but a damaged and ailing man, full of ill-advised precautions against the imaginary illnesses that were his interpretation of a general *malaise*. As much as anything he was homesick for Italy. He was not actively writing then, but he had two or three great Latin tomes in which he read and dreamt, he was annotating the works of Cassiodorus, edicts and proclamations and letters written for Theodoric the Goth, and full of light upon the manners and daily life of the time. And as the friends wandered in the Devonshire lanes or along the red Devonshire cliffs he talked of Italy. His friends had not seen Italy. To all three of them Italy was as far almost as it had been for all the English world in 1900. There was a day when they sat together by Lulworth Cove. He had been mourning the Italy he fancied he would never see again, and then he drew suddenly from his pocket an old pocket-book, and showed, treasured as one treasures the little things of those we love, a few scraps of paper that journey had left him: the empty cover of his railway tickets home, a flattened blossom from Hadrian's villa, a ticket for the Vatican Library, were chief among these things. He spoke as one speaks of a lost paradise. Yet before another year was over he had been through those experiences he has told so perfectly in *By the Ionian Sea*, and all three of these friends had met again in Rome. In Rome he had forgotten most of his illnesses; he went about proudly as one goes about one's dearly-loved native city. There were tramps in the Campagna, in the Alban Hills, along the Via Clodia, and so forth, merry meals with the good red wine of Velletri or Grotto Ferrata; and now the romance was more fully conceived, and in the Forum, on the Palatine Hill, upon the Appian Way, he could talk of the closing chapters that will never now be written—of Rome plague-stricken and deserted, Rome absolutely desolate under the fear of the Gothic king.[1]

[1] The following extract from a letter to Mr Edward Clodd is very characteristic of Gissing's attitude. It is dated Siena, 6

Many things were to happen to delay his new beginning, and, among others, there was in himself a certain diffidence before the new medium. But the spell of that Balzac-like sequence was already lifted from his mind. He had been persuaded, I believe by Mr Clement K. Shorter, to attempt short stories and sketches; he had attained to the completest mastery of his own proper qualities in the Calabrian travel-book already mentioned, and he was writing that frank, natural, and able study of Dickens that still waits for its just meed of recognition. Then there was *The [Private] Papers of Henry Ryecroft*, an experiment in the manner of Amiel's diary, that gave an interesting but one-sided sketch of the mental attitude to nature and contemporary things. He wrote, indeed, several more books in his earlier manner, but they made no marked advance upon *Eve's Ransom, Born in Exile*, and *The Year of Jubilee*, the first perhaps the best and the least appreciated of his novels. And at last, in the little village of St Jean Pied de Port, in the Pyrenees, he set himself to his long-delayed task. In October of last year he was in full work upon it and drawing near the end; he was in better health than he had

November 1897. "Of course I have not been able to see very much of Siena, but this is not *my* part of Italy. I have—I am sorry to say—comparatively little interest in the Renaissance. On the other hand, I shout with joy whenever I am brought very near to the old Romans. Chiefly I am delighted here with the magnificent white oxen, with huge horns, which draw carts about the streets. Oxen and carts are precisely those of Virgil."

been for many years, and tasting once again the pleasure of living. His letters to England were full of his romance. In his last, written on 28 November 1903, within a month of his end, he says: "I labour on at *Veranilda*, and, thank Heaven! have done more than three-fourths of it. I cannot judge whether it is good or bad, but the work has been severe—never more than a page a day at two sittings." A page in his microscopic handwriting was, in printer's language, a thousand words. He seems to have been at work upon the book before. In a letter dated 28 February 1901, he writes: "My sixth-century story keeps me amid old things. I seldom have time to look at any writing of the day," and in a letter, dated Arcachon, 8 January 1902, "My Roman novel, alas! is suspended by the state of my health, a little also, I admit, by the reflection that so many people have of late written novels about Rome." From St Pied de Port, so late as 10 June 1903, he says: "I have decided to write my sixth-century story. For the moment I turn with disgust from modern life, whereas these old times call to me with a pleasant voice. If I have anything like decent health here (which, by the by, is quite near to Roncesvalles) I *must* get this book done. I think I can make it fairly good, for I have saturated myself with the spirit of the age. It ought to be infinitely picturesque." And on 11 October 1903, he reports progress. "Well, I am getting on with my book. I am now well past the middle of *Veranilda*, and hope (with trembling) that I may finish by the end of the year. I don't think it will be bad; at all events, it gives me a certain pleasure in the writing. But it is harder work than any I ever did—not a line that does not ask sweat of the brain."

There is the shadow of prophecy in that "with trembling." At last but four chapters remained; and then came a cold, came pneumonia, and with the effect of a swift misadventure the end. In the last hours of his ebb and exhaustion he talked constantly of Veranilda, and of armour and weapons of the Goths.

And this book, *Veranilda*, that is so much of George Gissing, is unfinished, indeed, and unrevised, but so far done that even the end for his two principal characters, the Princess and Basil, is practically told. The book exists as a unity and as a whole, its truncation withdraws nothing essential from the design. One has one's minor uncertainties of course; what sinister treasure was to reward the search of Sagaris and Stephanus, what fate lurked ready to spring upon the Lady Heliodora and the reasons of the Lady Aurelia's long absence from the stage. But the main threads run clear to their end; in a moment the tumult of the assailing Goths, terrible by reason of their massacre at Tibur, would have become audible, and the wave of panic that left Rome to the dogs and vermin have swept us to the end. And the end was morning, a sunlit silence upon the empty Forum, upon the as yet unruined Palatine Hill, upon the yet unshattered Basilica of Constantine. For just that one tremendous moment in her history Rome lay still.

But in spite of all that is lacking this romance exists sufficiently for its total effect, and one sees for the first time clearly what indeed *The Whirlpool* and *The Year of Jubilee* went far to suggest to the experienced critic, and that is George Gissing's extraordinary power of comprehensive design. All the characters move living to a synthesis of impression. It is the picture of a magnificent decay—of the last days, of the last hours of the tradition of Imperial Rome. Every figure partakes of that transition and is significant in the scheme: the sombre figure of the dying Maximus, with which the book begins; the ragged Decius, with his unenvied treasure of manuscripts, with his whispered doubts whether, after all, Virgil's Fourth Ecologue was a prophecy of Christ; the deacon Leander, incessant and acquisitive, politic, blindly devoted, building up the wealth and power of the Mediaeval Church amidst a universal ruin; the senator, Venatius, a senator half-way changed to a feudal lord, fortifying his country villa, are of the many who were preparing the way for the final disintegration. Then one marks the Lady Petronilla, obsessed by religious ambition, the wretched Marcian, torn between the new fear of hell that had come into the world and the immemorial desire of the flesh; and Basil, setting aside the old Roman dignity, reviling the old training in rhetoric and letters and giving his mind to arms. All things, with an art of imperceptible touches, display a time when security had gone, while still the tradition of empire, of a wide law and government, the afterglow of the classical civilisation, haunted the broken bridges, the fresh-shattered aqueducts, the rutted, vacant ways. Even to the smallest details the picture is complete. Let the reader note the source of the lead for the coffin of Maximus, the prey on the cart of the passing lime-burner, the waterless uncleanliness that heralded the pest. It needs some practice in the art of imaginative writing to gauge quite how skilfully this magnificent conception has been wrought, to detect the subtle insistence, touch by touch, that keeps its mellow and melancholy atmosphere true. The whole learning that was possible at this period lies behind this book, yet there is no heaviness, no impressive jabbering of strange terms, no hint of a claim to scholarship, none of the tricks that drive this sort of fact to recognition. Gissing carries his learning as a trained athlete carries his limbs, as it were, unwittingly, as a great artist saturated with the classical tradition might best desire to do. And he gains in permanence and beauty what he will lose in contemporary applause. Now at any rate he can bear to wait a little longer for the honour that will in the end be his in absolute security.

INDEX